THE ARTFUL MANAGER

E. Andrew Taylor

THE ARTFUL MANAGER

FIELD NOTES ON THE BUSINESS OF ARTS AND CULTURE

The Artful Manager:
Field Notes on the Business of Arts and Culture
by E. Andrew Taylor

2021

arts axis press
Washington, DC
artsaxis.com

ISBN (paperback): 978-1-7368585-0-9
ISBN (Apple Book): 978-1-7368585-1-6
ISBN (Kindle): 978-1-7368585-2-3

Interior Book Design: Sue Balcer
Cover Photo: Earl Wilcox on Unsplash
Back Cover Photo: Pinho . on Unsplash

Dedicated to the brilliant and beautiful humans
who make artistic expression and experience more possible,
more present, and more connected.

CONTENTS

PROLOGUE

Folklorist and writer Zora Neale Hurston defined research as "formalized curiosity," as "poking and prying with a purpose."[1] For many researchers, "field notes" capture the sketches, clippings, scraps, tidbits, and scrawls through which that poking and prying takes shape.

In July 2003, at the kind and compelling invitation of Doug McLennan at ArtsJournal.com, I began writing my own "field notes" through the then-evolving medium of a blog. I was about eight years into my teaching career in nonprofit arts management, discovering (as teaching forces you to discover) the magnitude of what I didn't know or understand about the field I had come to love.

The "purpose" that drove me was a nagging intuition that while the language, lenses, and assumptions of arts management may serve the work, they also distort our view and disrupt our progress. The charge I wrote as a first field note still captures the gist of that suspicion:

> For six decades now, nonprofit arts and culture organizations have focused on a corporate ideal. Using the mantras of for-profit America – effectiveness, efficiency, professionalism, best practices, change management, accountability – a generation of arts leaders has struggled to graft business basics onto the world of creative expression.

> But what if, all along the way, we fundamentally misunderstood what it meant to be run "like a business"? What if our management metaphors actually contribute to the problems we hope they will solve – separateness, disengagement, inflexibility, inequity, entropy, and stress?
>
> The Artful Manager seeks a new set of metaphors for administrative leaders of arts and culture. There is a need for business thinking, to be sure, with an intensity and deftness we have only begun to understand. But there is also an energy beyond money and markets that the artful manager must channel. What if, in the end, the arts organization is not a problem to be managed, but an instrument to be played?[2]

This book gathers 50 posts from the first 18 years of my online field notes – edited, updated, complemented with opening quotes, and sorted into three themes.

In revising these works, I was filled again with gratitude and humility for the constellation of brilliant, beautiful, and inspiring people who read and reacted to them; who helped me think, speak, and act in the world in more productive ways; and who shaped me as a teacher, learner, and ally for the creative humans I love so dearly.

Here's hoping these field notes bring some similar value to your own poking and prying, and to the valiant and vibrant work you do in the arts.

MANAGEMENT PRACTICE

1

ACT LIKE A BUSINESS? WHY AIM SO LOW?

"There's no business like show business."
IRVING BERLIN

In his monograph, *Good to Great and the Social Sectors,* Jim Collins makes a rather bold statement: "We must reject the idea – well-intentioned, but dead wrong – that the primary path to greatness in the social sectors is to become 'more like a business.'"[3] His point is that most businesses are poorly run, and that many business practices correlate with mediocrity, not greatness. So, to him, telling nonprofit organizations to "run like a business" is like telling artists to lower their standards, or telling a visionary leader to "aim low."

For those of us who have been struggling to convince cultural leaders to work with more focus, more discipline, and more responsiveness, Collins' words come as a bit of a blow. But I must admit he has a point. For the past decades, our industry has fundamentally misunderstood what it means to run "like a business." As a result, we've tended to become more rigid, less joyous, and increasingly disconnected from the communities and the creative spirit we were formed to serve.

In the Arts Management master's degree program where I teach, we get to see both sides of the question – dwelling in management theory and practice, and working every day with cultural nonprofits. From that perspective, I suggest a six-point alternative to "running like a business," to give arts leaders more worthy targets:

> *Strive to be better than a business.* Being responsible, accountable, transparent, and responsive is the lowest standard we should set for ourselves. Let's be exceptional.
>
> *Use business tools with an artist's hand.* Business tools are merely ways to see the world, and ways to structure our interaction with it. Let's be like the artists among us and around us and explore those tools with creative abandon.
>
> *Embrace our roles as social engineers.* So much of our work involves engineering compelling social experiences and catalytic community space. Let's learn the tools of those trades with the same energy and effort we commit to our more familiar tasks.
>
> *Define our own goals, rather than having them assigned to us.* We are continually lured by outside measures of success: economic impact, educational enhancement, social service. If these are our goals,

let's embrace them. If not, let's clarify our purpose to our constituents and ourselves.

Work with clarity and discipline. Nonprofit arts organizations don't have the luxury of elbow room; every action must be taken with elegance, intent, and an openness to learn and improve.

Calculate our efforts in multiple currencies. There are a multitude of resources beyond money that drive what we do: joy, discovery, connection, sense of purpose, sense of place, and on and on. Let's make room in our spreadsheets and strategic plans to ensure we're measuring what matters.

In the end, behaving "like a business" is a matter of semantics. Arts organizations are businesses, so their behavior is businesslike – just as good or just as bad. The deeper question is what kind of business do you want to be? And what skills and perspective do you need to get there? It's not about mimicry. It's about clarity, curiosity, and courage.

A version of this article originally appeared in the July/August 2006 issue of Inside Arts.

2

THINKING AND SPEAKING

"I...never could make a good impromptu speech without several hours to prepare it."

MARK TWAIN

Most of us have been admonished from an early age to "think before you speak." But it turns out that speaking doesn't work that way. Studies in psycholinguistics (Smith and Wheeldon 1999,[4] for example) suggest that humans routinely dive into spoken sentences without a plan for how they will end. We do some basic preprocessing of the opening phrase, and perhaps some sketching around how it might end. But otherwise, we're constructing the sentence as we say it. Just notice yourself speaking at some moment today and see what you do.

Normally, an author would get normative after that statement: saying you should think a whole sentence through before you say it. But that's not how our brains work. And if they did, we'd never actually speak to each other in productive ways.

Spoken communication is constructed entirely in context and in response to a thousand variables – implicit and explicit. Leaping into a sentence before it's fully constructed is a necessary fact of life. And when you think of it, it's also an extraordinary act of faith – that the rest of the sentence will be waiting for you when you get to it; that you have a passable working knowledge of vocabulary, grammar, and syntax to make it through mostly unscathed; and that the person you're speaking to will be a collaborative partner in unpacking whatever you construct.

By this metric, each of us is making a thousand small leaps of faith each day.

This disconnect, between what we're supposed to do before speaking and what we actually do, strikes me as relevant to the many ways we talk about strategy and planning. We're supposed to draft a thorough plan before taking action in our individual work, or the collective work of our organization. We're supposed to think through all contingencies, and plan for them.

But what we actually do, at our best, is think through the opening phrase, and the possible closing phrase, and dive in. So many of the managers I meet in arts organizations recognize this in their work and feel bad about it. They imagine that they should have a better plan for their day, week, month, or year. But they're mostly acting in faith, and in response to the moments they bump into. As a result, they self-criticize continually, even as they're diving in to do extraordinary work.

The insights of psycholinguistics tell us we can't and won't prepare our sentences in full before we begin them.

But we can and might build our capacity to construct them on the fly. We can improve our vocabulary, enhance our focus and attention, listen more deeply, read sentences by masters to hear and feel how they flow. And, we can be open to our own voice and what it's reaching for mid-sentence, kindly encourage it along, and forgive it when it inevitably wanders off the path.

As E.M. Forster framed it: "Think before you speak is criticism's motto; speak before you think is creation's."[5]

Original blog post: September 26, 2016

3
NOTICING AND JUDGING

"If you want the truth to stand clear before you, never be for or against. The struggle between 'for' and 'against' is the mind's worst disease."

SENT-TS'AN, C. 700 CE

One of the attributes we recognize and admire in great artists, curators, and other professionals is how quickly and decisively they assess the world around them. They see almost immediately whether an action, object, or direction is "right" or "aligned" with some larger vision. Or whether an action, object, or direction is "good" by technical or aesthetic standards.

It is, in part, this ability to judge in the moment that makes their work exceptional. Through fast and focused assessment, they make continual micro and macro adjustments to what they're doing. And the process finds its way to beauty, power, or impact because they and their team are able to make these adjustments in ways the rest of us cannot fathom or perceive.

Because this is a celebrated quality of great artists, craftspeople, and other professionals, it is natural to assume that the path to greatness is about judging more quickly and more decisively. We should determine "right" or "good" as fast as we can, and then say it as loudly as we can, with commitment.

This is a rookie mistake.

In fact, what we perceive to be fast and focused judgment in extraordinary people is (usually) the byproduct of thousands of hours of suspended judgment...time spent learning to pause and probe an observation or experience long enough to understand it, and also to understand its relationship to a vision or goal.

What we perceive as instinct is more like relentlessly disciplined muscle memory or mental habit.

So, if your goal is greatness – peak performance in whatever it is you care about doing – fast and furious isn't the place to begin. The place to begin is to notice without judgment – to see, and to say what you see, as cleanly as possible, without bundled assumptions.

This may sound stupid and dull. But this is how mastery begins – in art, in business, in pretty much anything. And this is how judgment actually gets better, and eventually faster.

Learn to notice without judgment (at least at first). From what I've noticed, it's the best first step toward greatness.

Original blog post: November 5, 2015

4

OTHER PEOPLE'S METRICS

"We try to measure what we value. We come to value what we measure."
DONELLA MEADOWS

I'm part of a lot of conversations about metrics and measurement in the arts – the various ways we look for evidence that we're making progress on mission, or making a difference in some area of our community. And for many I speak with, metrics are a matter of concern and frustration: Why must I shift my focus from the work to measure the impact of the work? Or, why must I bend my artistic vision to achieve some external measure?

My response is becoming increasingly consistent: You *don't* have to do those things...as long as you're not asking for other people's money.

As soon as you take someone else's dollar – whether a donor or a foundation or a ticket buyer or a taxpayer (via a public agency) – you are suddenly subject to their metrics of success...particularly if you want *another* dollar after the one you just received.

Of course, their metrics might include joy and creation and escape and wonder. Or their metrics might include employment statistics, property values, public education, and success of surrounding retail. Your job as a cultural leader is to understand the various expectations that came with the money or time or attention, and to show you are meeting those expectations (while still staying true to your artistic or community mission).

You may not like that job. But you accepted that job when you accepted that dollar.

I'm constantly attempting to define the boundaries of the industry I study and serve. The "nonprofit arts" isn't quite right, as it's too narrow. Nor is the "arts and culture industries" sufficient, as it seems too broad. My working definition is this:

> Enterprises that require more than one person to accomplish, that claim creative human expression as a primary purpose, and that can't or choose not to recapture their full costs from the audience they seek to serve.

Those enterprises *require* other people's money. And other people's money comes bundled with other people's metrics.

Original blog post: October 3, 2012

5
AESTHETIC ATTENTION

"We don't see things as they are,
we see them as we are."
ANAÏS NIN

Arts organizations are in the business of aesthetic experience. I hope this isn't a radical statement, but an obvious point. Whether the organization is fostering work by artists, connecting that work to audiences, or preserving that work for now and forever, the core of the matter is the aesthetic connection between an observer and a creative action or object.

So what, exactly, constitutes an aesthetic experience? And how might we behave as artists, audiences, and managers to make such experience more possible and more profound?

Fortunately for all of us, this isn't a new or unusual question. And many have attempted to answer it (not many in arts management[6]...but we tend to borrow from others anyway). Philosopher Monroe Beardsley offered a particularly useful attempt in an essay on the subject, where he suggested five "criteria of the aesthetic character of experience."[7]

> *Object Directedness*
> A willing focus of attention on the object or activity.
>
> *Felt Freedom*
> Release from concerns about past and future. Feeling "lost in the moment."
>
> *Detached Affect*
> The sense of the object or activity being at a slight distance from our emotions, even though it may spark deep emotions.
>
> *Active Discovery*
> An animated sense of our mind or our emotions at work, seeking and finding patterns or connections.
>
> *Wholeness*
> Feeling integrated as a person (self-acceptance, self-expansion), and/or feeling the work is coherent and whole itself, that all the parts are "of a piece."

Beardsley proposed that "aesthetic experience" requires the first criteria along with at least three of the others.

Those who are familiar with Mihaly Csikszentmihalyi's characteristics of "flow experience" will recognize many similar themes...even though aesthetics is a focus of philosophy while flow is a focus of psychology (and the two threads were developed independently).[8]

If we accept these criteria for "aesthetic experience" (which I'm guessing many of you don't want to, but go with the flow for the moment), then we can imagine aspects of "aesthetic attention" that might help each of us explore and enhance such experience, and help others do so too. These might include:

Intentional Attention
Bringing energy and effort to what we are observing, and how we are doing so.

Softened Judgment / Discernment over Deciding
Relaxing into our observation to delay our reflex to decide (see "Noticing before Knowing").

Compassionate Detachment
Observing the object, action, or process at a slight distance (retaining empathy), as an "object of creative attention."

Relentless Curiosity
Leaning into the unknown and complex, responding to challenging discoveries with inquiry rather than fear.

Systems Thinking
Perception of the whole as well as the parts.

If arts organizations are about aesthetic experience, perhaps arts managers should develop and exercise aesthetic attention – not only in their view of the work they support and connect, but also in the processes and practices they use every day. Of course, they should also be extraordinary craftspeople of business and collective action. But might they also be active advocates for the aesthetic?

Original blog post: February 17, 2016

6

UNDER CONTRACT WITH THE PUBLIC TRUST

"Society is indeed a contract. It is a partnership in all science; a partnership in all art; a partnership in every virtue, and in all perfection. As the ends of such a partnership cannot be obtained in many generations, it becomes a partnership not only between those who are living, but between those who are living, those who are dead, and those who are to be born."

EDMUND BURKE

Anyone who does business with anyone will likely know the essential elements of a valid contract: valid offer, valid acceptance, intention to create legal relations, and consideration. But we don't often realize how many interconnecting contracts we are a party to: personal service contracts (mobile phone, Internet, utilities, mortgage, auto lease), business contracts (with suppliers, banks, employees, and such). We buy or sell tickets to performances or events, which are contracts, as well.

Current economic theory suggests that the organizations we work in and contract with are, themselves, only bundles of contracts. Says the classic 1976 article by Michael C. Jensen and William H. Meckling:

> ...most organizations are simply legal fictions which serve as a nexus for a set of contracting relationships among individuals.[9]

And yet there's one essential contract we seem to forget about in the nonprofit arts – the contract that defines our relationship with the public trust. We talk in the United States about nonprofit status being "granted" or "given" by the Internal Revenue Service. But really, it's a binding contract between our organizations and the public.

> There's a *valid offer*: Our articles of incorporation, bylaws, and filing documents, all of which promise that we'll do things only charitable organizations would do.
>
> There's a *valid acceptance*: The designation of our non-stock corporate status from the state, and the "letter of determination" from the Internal Revenue Service.
>
> There's an *intention to create legal relations*: The stacks of signed documents and forms we shuttle back and forth with our state government and the IRS upon our formation, and in required reporting thereafter.

> And, of course, there's *consideration*: For the organization, there's a bundle of fiscal benefits including contributed income free of taxation by the donor, exemption from various taxes, discount postage, and the like. For the IRS, representing the public, there's our promise of charitable behavior as well as the promise not to do things that aren't in line with charitable purpose.

That's a contract. The IRS and state are, essentially, the trustees representing the public. Our nonprofit governing board is the trustee representing the organization, responsible for proper execution of the promises made.

So often, when I hear arts or service organizations talk about nonprofit corporate status, it sounds like a bundle of benefits they've been given because their work is special or worthy. But, really, it's a contract. It carries consideration for both sides. And therefore, it comes at a cost to the organization (that we hope is equal to its benefits).

There's a rolling conversation about what the consideration should be for nonprofit status in the arts – that nonprofit arts organizations owe it to the public to be more diverse, more risk-taking, less commercial, more engaged with their communities. But the particular nature of this contractual relationship is that the organization gets to define how their work serves the public trust, and the organization's donors, supporters, its state's attorney general, and the IRS get to decide whether that definition is sufficient.

That said, if an organization doesn't express and explain how it lives up to its part of the contract, it leaves the question open for others to interpret. And if an organization, or its board, forgets that it's part of a binding agreement, it's stepping dangerously toward breach of contract.

Original blog post: June 21, 2013

7

NOT ALL QUESTIONS ARE EQUAL

"Don't search for the answers, which could not be given to you now, because you would not be able to live them. And the point is, to live everything. Live the questions now. Perhaps then, someday far in the future, you will gradually, without even noticing it, live your way into the answer."

RANIER MARIA RILKE

I have learned that a question is almost always the best approach: to begin something, to welcome someone, to unlock a stubborn problem, to enlist enduring support, to launch a difficult conversation, or to become a part of a community rather than standing apart.

In a world of declarations that define boundaries, a question is an invitation to cross boundaries. In a room full of strong opinions, a question is a disarming force that can open minds. When I've found the courage to ask a question – especially when every impulse in me wants to judge, accuse, dismiss, instruct, conclude, correct, or just disappear – I've been grateful for it. And yet, I'm still learning my own advice.

In the spectrum of possible questions, though, not all are created equal. Among the lower forms to avoid are:

> The "look how smart I am" question, a common preening behavior at conferences, where the point is to boast a personal victory rather than build a conversation.
>
> The "look how dumb you are" question, intended to be cruel, embarrassing, or belittling.
>
> The loaded question, piled high with narrow facts and fancy rhetoric to defend your current opinion.

The best questions (like the best leaders) are genuine, generous, and courageous. Genuine, in that they signal a true interest in learning from the response. Generous, in that they offer focused space for someone else to speak. Courageous, because bold questions make you vulnerable – to attention, dismissal, or the frightening insight that you don't know everything.

Most of all, ask questions of yourself. When tempted to blame or belittle yourself, or something you've done, or something you can't bring yourself to do, ask a genuine, generous, and courageous question instead. And invite yourself into a useful conversation.

We all deserve that kind of respect.

Originally written for Barry Hessenius' blog for his "What I've Learned" collection, September 22, 2003.

8

THE PYRAMID AND THE WHEEL

"For within structures defined by profit, by linear power, by institutional dehumanization, our feelings were not meant to survive."

AUDRE LORDE

There are countless ways to categorize collective human action (by legal entity, by sector, by structure, by tax status, by geography, and on and on). But sociologist/historian Johan Galtung suggests there are essentially two ways we organize ourselves: thick-and-small ("the wheel" or "Beta") and thin-and-big ("the pyramid" or "Alpha").[10]

In Galtung's framing, the "small/big" distinction describes the size of the collective. The line between small and big collectives is "roughly the upper limit to the number of people a human being can identify, and relate to, positively and negatively." According to anthropologist Robin Dunbar, that number is somewhere between 100 and 250 people, with 150 often used as a useful placeholder.[11]

Galtung's "thick/thin" distinction refers to the nature of relationships within the structure. "Thick" interactive relations are particular, personal, specific, and therefore unique to each relationship. They can't be substituted or exchanged. Think here about immediate family, close friends, small villages, or close associates in your social network. "Thin" interactive relations are more universal, functional, and even generic. Think here about professional relationships based on job title or function (or military rank or ownership status or other "type"), where the person may change but the role relationship will remain much the same.

Obviously, "pyramid" structures can and do contain "wheel" structures within them (tight-knit working groups, for example, or friend groups). But you can't get "big" without also favoring "thin" relationships as a dominant practice.

Galtung attributes much of the rise of modern society to the development and dominance of "thin-and-big" structures: corporations, bureaucracies, institutional religion, and the like. He says that these "have provided us with material abundance and impressive control and coordination structures." However, he says, pyramid (Alpha) structures tend to crowd out and even dissolve wheel (Beta) structures, because, in part:

> Alpha requires full attention, because the jobs provided by Alpha are full time jobs, and because the occupants of Alpha positions are not supposed to think Beta thoughts.

There's lots to unbundle in this, including the larger "anomie and atomie" in our society that Galtung attributes to the pyramid. But my immediate point is more narrow.

So many of our structural, managerial, and organizational assumptions in the nonprofit arts are drawn from "the pyramid" or the "thin-and-big" (stable job titles, hierarchies, departments, detached professional relationships, and so on). But the vast majority of arts nonprofits are radically small.[12] It's a rare arts organization that has a staff larger than 150, and most have staff of five or less.[13]

The pyramid offers unprecedented size, scale, and geographic spread. But it comes at a dramatic cost to the human soul and psyche. Still, many arts organizations pay that cost without thinking, and without actually needing what it buys.

Further, the pyramid is not only a mismatch to the scale of arts nonprofits, it's also a mismatch to their function. Creative production is essentially collaborative, human-centric, relationship-based, and highly specific to the individual members of the team. Here again, the pyramid tends to crush this kind of culture, rather than nurture it.

Arts leader and educator Aaron Dworkin once shared that when a new individual joined his organization, they wouldn't introduce the new person to the existing team. They would introduce *everyone* to the *new* team. "Because any one person changes the entire system and changes the entire team."[14] That's one of the many things a wheel organization would do. How else might you reimagine your own organization as a wheel rather than a pyramid?

Original blog post: May 30, 2018

9

ACCESSIBLE OR HOSPITABLE

"...I try to create a hospitable tone at the beginning of a poem. Stepping from the title to the first lines is like stepping into a canoe. A lot of things can go wrong."
BILLY COLLINS

We talk a lot in the arts about being "accessible" – which tends to mean open and available to many different people. The assumption (and often the experience) is that a lot of artistic work is difficult to approach and challenging to engage, whether in the content itself, or in the places and practices around it. A frequent reaction to the word "accessible" is that it means "dumbing down" the work, making it less rich, less complex, and less unique so that more people will consume it. That leads conversations to an impasse.

Poet Billy Collins has an on-going skirmish with the word "accessible," which is often used to describe his work. Because his poems are full of plain language and wry humor, many find them easier to approach than the poems of his more cryptic counterparts. But Collins isn't fond of the word, telling PBS:

> I think accessible just means that the reader can walk into the poem without difficulty. The poem is not, as someone put it, deflective of entry. But the real question is what happens to the reader once he or she gets inside the poem? That's the real question for me... getting the reader into the poem and then taking the reader somewhere because I think of poetry as a kind of...travel writing.[15]

Instead, Collins prefers the word "hospitable." Says he to *Paris Review*:

> There is no pre-existing reason for you to be interested in me and certainly not in my family, so there must be a lure at the beginning of a poem. I want the reader to be in the sidecar, ready. Then off we go. Then we can take a ride from what seemed to be a hospitable and friendly environment into an environment that's perhaps disorienting, manipulative, or a little off-balancing. I want to start in a very familiar place and end up in a strange place.[16]

Hospitable poems are no less rich, complex, murky, joyful, evocative, or dark. They just welcome you from where you are, and invite you in. As he tells *The Observer*, "Poetry is a mix of clarity and mystery. It's important to know when to be clear and when to be mysterious. Too much fog is bad. Too much mist."[17]

While I'm not interested or authorized to tell artists how to make their work, I do a bit of business with the professionals and organizations that connect that work to the world. And there I think that Collins' approach can carry us to a better conversation about arts experiences. It's not necessarily about being "accessible" – like one of those easy-off/easy-on gas stations on the interstate. It's not about pandering or being palatable. It's about being attentive to the anxiety or apprehension of your guest, letting them know they're welcome and they're seen. It's about being hospitable, a gracious and generous host for the rich (and challenging) journey ahead.

NOTE: "Accessible" here does NOT refer to the significant issue of "accessibility," the active removal of physical, sensory, and cognitive barriers that block access to a location or an experience. However, the two are deeply intertwined, and both require a commitment to open awareness and open arms.

Original blog post: April 6, 2017

10
FOUR FUNCTIONS/ DYSFUNCTIONS OF MANAGERS

"She said
you could measure a life in as many ways
as there were to bake a pound cake,
but you still needed real butter and eggs
for a good one – pound cake, that is,
but I knew what she meant."

RITA DOVE

A former professor of mine used to say that there are two kinds of people in the world: those who divide the world into kinds of people, and those who don't. Now as a professor myself, I would add a third kind: those who cautiously categorize but feel bad about it. That would be me. Faced with seemingly random complexity, it can be handy to group behaviors and tendencies (not people), but only for a specific and time-limited problem at hand, and only if you feel wary all along the way.

The "problem at hand" for me, as a faculty member in Arts Management, is how to define, describe, develop, and direct management capacity with my students, and how to observe it in useful ways in the working world. For that problem, management scholar and consultant Ichak Adizes has a rather simple but functional sorting approach.

In his book, *Leading the Leaders,*[18] Adizes suggests that there are four essential roles of a manager, and that nobody excels at them all. Most of us have one or two dominant roles, just as most of us have a dominant hand. Rather than striving toward one perfect person (since the roles can be incompatible with each other), Adizes suggests we strive toward more balanced and integrated teams that can work with and across different roles and worldviews.

In brief, the four management roles Adizes defines are:

> *Producer (P)*: Deliver and execute the task at hand, ensure immediate-term results, know what needs to happen and get it done…right now.
>
> *Administrator (A)*: Develop and defend organizational processes, ensure efficiency in the short run, forsee the problems, barriers, or procedural issues behind ideas and consider how systems might (or might not) navigate them.
>
> *Entrepreneur (E)*: Discover long-term changes and opportunities, set a vision, see through the fog of a hazy future and describe a next reality.
>
> *Integrator (I)*: Connect and nourish collective spirit, build capacity for teamwork and shared decision-making, find and weave together common threads.

If you were particularly strong in the Administrator role, Adizes would code you as a pAei. If you predominantly thought and worked from a Producer perspective, he would label you a Paei. Again, according to Adizes, while you might have two areas of strength, a fully-balanced PAEI doesn't exist in the wild, even though much management theory and training strives for such a person.

A handy byproduct of Adizes' simple model is that it not only defines the functions of managers, but also the likely dysfunctions that occur when a manager is hyper-dominant in one area – without empathy or appreciation for any other area. These come with catchy titles that will likely remind you of former bad bosses:

> *The Lone Ranger* (or the Lone Wolf) is the extreme form of the Producer, who focuses exclusively on immediate work, trusts nobody else to do that work, and thrives on a desk piled high with projects. When faced with outcomes that don't match expectation, the Lone Ranger doubles down – doing exactly the same thing only twice as hard.

> *The Bureaucrat* is the extreme form of the Administrator, who cares exclusively about how things get done, and whether they're done according to policy and administrative practice. Prefers to do things right rather than doing the right things.

> *The Arsonist* is the extreme form of the Entrepreneur, eager to burn down any current practice, process, or product in search of a bold future idea. Often

> charismatic and compelling, the Arsonist is toxic to thoughtful, sustainable, collaborative enterprise.
>
> *The SuperFollower* is the extreme form of the Integrator, desperate for consensus and calm at the expense of forward motion or difficult change. Will never say what they want or think, but only ask what you or others want or think.

All of these, of course, are cartoons. Adizes' entire framework is extremely broad, a radical rough-cut/short-cut through highly complex human behaviors and belief systems. But that's a large part of its utility (at least for me). The goal isn't to label with permanent ink, but to highlight key tendencies that might need attention, and to encourage awareness of difference across a working team.

While these frames and approaches may be useful, it's important to remember (constantly) that they are flawed. There aren't two kinds of people. There aren't four kinds of managers. There aren't seven habits of highly effective people. There are humans, doing their best, who can sometimes learn from a signpost, a rough sketch, a caricature, or a metaphor. Use such things with care and compassion. Some assembly required.

Original blog post: June 28, 2017

11

THE SHALLOW BREATHING OF RATIONAL MANAGEMENT

"Breathe with unconditional breath
the unconditioned air."
WENDELL BERRY

So much of our training, theory, practice, and focus in cultural management has to do with outcomes and processes. When we look to improve how our organizations "work," we tend to choose between "making better things" (the outcomes or products), or "making things better" (the processes that lead to those outcomes).

This is not a bad way to spend our time, but it's incomplete. And it tends to leave so many arts professionals feeling short of time, short of breath, and short of energy.

In short (see what I did there?), we feel like we're shallow-breathing, moving air at a rapid pace but not getting much oxygen.

This issue is not unique to arts organizations, but it's particularly salient to the arts. The great waves of management theory and practice in the wider world have moved through the same attention deficits: First came product-market-output focus (in the 1950s, '60s, '70s), where managers differentiated functions within the company, established performance metrics (such as KPIs or Key Performance Indicators), and adjusted their work toward better outputs. Then came process-focused management theory and practice (in the 1980s and 1990s) in the form of Total Quality Management (TQM), organizational learning, workflow analysis, and other forms of midstream attention.

In systems thinking, we would call the products/outputs "stocks" – buckets of nouns that can be counted (staff levels, event nights, sales, dollars, inventory). Processes would be called "flows" – the pipeline verbs that define our activities (hiring, building, training, selling). Attending to both is essential work if you want to grow, learn, and improve over time. But attending *only* to those two leaves out a rather important bit of the plumbing: the source or the wellspring.

The wellspring for any enterprise is the deep, human, driving force that compels both output and process. It's not what you do at work, or how, but rather *why* you're there in the first place. This *why* is often deeper than rational reasoning, and beyond traditional management language.

C. Otto Scharmer describes these three layers of attention and intention in his book *Theory U*, making it clear that every layer is essential to a healthy enterprise. He describes the three layers as an organic whole, with healthy leaders and managers "breathing" deeply – in from products through processes to source, then back out again from source to processes to products. Says he:

> The point is not to argue for an upstream point of view of leadership at the expense of processes, capabilities, and execution, but to conceive of the whole field of leading and organizing as a single living entity, one that is grounded in and constantly renewed from the source of attention and intention at the center.... The center does not exist without the periphery, and vice versa.[19]

So, if you find yourself feeling short of breath, after hours of attention on the products or the processes of your organization's work: stop. Take a deep breath, and invite your colleagues to breathe as well, to return your attention to the reasons you're there in the first place. Then let your change or improvement efforts flow back out from there.

Original blog post: September 6, 2017

12

THE BUDGET GAMES

"May the odds be ever in your favor."
EFFIE TRINKET (via SUZANNE COLLINS)

The budgeting or project funding process in any organization is often imagined as a game of reason, logic, and responsible collaboration, but experienced as a miniature *Hunger Games.* The allocation of resources shapes and is shaped by the power, privileges, and priorities of an enterprise. So it's no wonder that budgeting is such a hothouse for politics and sneaky persuasion.

In his classic (and strangely expensive) book, *Overcoming Organizational Defenses,*[20] management scholar Chris Argyris offers a fabulous list of 12 budget games managers and politicians play when trying to get a project passed through the system.

To my eye, these games look eerily familiar both to internal organizational budgeting and also to external arguments for individual, philanthropic, and public support for the arts. See how many look familiar to your terrain or toolbox (be honest):

Foot in the door
Sell a new program modestly. Conceal its real magnitude.

Hidden ball
Conceal a politically unattractive program within an attractive one.

Divide and conquer
Seek approval of a budget request from more than one supervisor.

Distraction
Base a specific request on the premise that an overall program has been approved when this is not in fact the case.

It's free
Argue that someone else will pay for the project so the organization might as well approve it.

Razzle-dazzle
Support the request with voluminous data, but arranged in such a way that their significance is not clear.

Delayed buck
Submit the data late, arguing that the budget guidelines required so much detailed calculation that the job could not be done on time.

Our program is priceless
It is difficult to argue against defense or human life.

It can't be measured
The real benefit is subjective.

Tomorrow and tomorrow
If there are no results today, promise some in the future.

Stretching things
The real skill is not simply to promise something that is difficult to prove; promise something that is impossible to disprove.

Both ends against the middle
Play competing committees against each other.

Let the games begin!

Original blog post: April 25, 2005

13
THE DESCENT INTO ORDER

"The Revolution evaporates, and leaves behind only the slime of a new bureaucracy."
FRANZ KAFKA

Anyone who took physics or wore a black turtleneck and smoked clove cigarettes will know about "entropy" – the tendency of a system to descend into disorder, to lose working energy over time. Entropy is the reason hot things cool down, and the reason philosophy students are such downers at parties.

But lately I've been wondering if there might be an opposite tendency for complex human systems (like arts organizations, and arts ecologies) that's equally deadening: a descent into order. Explosive, exploratory, innovative, and passionate groups begin an endeavor with a scramble for new approaches and an openness to new ideas. If successful in gathering resources and supporters, they often become rational, stable, process-focused, and risk-averse. They grow up. They calm down. They get organized and spend more of their available time getting even more organized – in large part because their funders tell them to.

Howard S. Becker, in *Art Worlds*, describes this very tendency in some arts ecosystems. Says he:

> The originally expressive art works and styles become increasingly more organized, constrained, and ritualized; organizational forms subordinate the artist increasingly to partially or entirely extraneous sources of control; and the world and its activities begin to resemble conventional craft worlds. In this sense, an art turns into a craft.[21]

Becker doesn't mean that "craft" is a lesser form of human expression, only that it's a different form with different rules, roles, and behaviors.

There are moments – admittedly, often just before I begin a new semester of teaching – when I wonder if the professional nonprofit arts ecology is trending this way (despite many examples of extraordinary, explosive efforts within it). I sense a growing emphasis on effectiveness and mechanics, and a descent away from dynamic and dramatic expression. And I wonder whether there's another way to think and work.

In *The Ideology of the Aesthetic*,[22] Terry Eagleton suggests three "great questions of philosophy," which seem a good place to start (the words within parentheses are mine):

> What can we know?" (which I'll associate with "reason" or "truth")

> "What ought we to do?" (which I'll associate with "ethics" or "goodness")
>
> "What do we find attractive?" (which I'll associate with "aesthetics" or "beauty")

In the evolving field of "organizational aesthetics" (yes, that's a thing), scholars and practitioners wonder whether those three domains may also be applicable to business. As John Dobson[23] frames the questions for business decisions:

> Is it profitable? (which I'd translate to "is it effective," among nonprofits)
>
> Is it ethical?
>
> Is it beautiful?

And while most management teams may blink at that final point, Dobson suggests that "when beauty is adequately defined, the third question becomes the most fundamental criterion of the three."

Entropy, philosophy, aesthetics…what the hell am I getting at? I'm getting at this:

I see an opportunity to rethink how we think, act, and learn about collective action in expressive endeavor (or "the arts" if you prefer). Order, reason, and effectiveness are essential, of course. But that particular type of order can dissipate creative and expressive energy over time.

What if we countered the "descent into order" not with disorder, but with *multiple* types of order: for a start, why not reason, ethics, and aesthetics...truth, goodness, and beauty? What if we approached the arts organization as an expressive endeavor in itself, as well as a tool to produce, present, and preserve expressive work? What would that look like? What attitudes and aptitudes would it require from its participants? And how might it change the game?

It may be time to bring beauty into organizational design, development, and management – especially in organizations whose very purpose is beauty. It's certainly time to explore that idea.

Original blog post: January 7, 2016

14
THE PROBLEM WITH PROBLEMS

"It isn't that they can't see the solution. It is that they can't see the problem."
G.K. CHESTERTON

If you work in the arts in higher education (or any education, for that matter), you are likely talking or hearing more about "complex problems," or perhaps "wicked problems." These are shorthand for a wide range of messy, persistent, usually negative aspects of civil or global society – hunger, inequity, racism, terrorism, climate change, sectarianism, and so on. And these phrases are the latest reason to value and integrate the arts.

The argument goes this way: The world has become more complex. Reason and rational knowledge aren't sufficient anymore. Rather, robust understanding and engagement with these problems require creativity, innovation, divergent thinking, and other magic mojo we claim for the arts.

I'll admit that I'm a proponent of such arguments. And I do believe that artistic process and practice have deep importance to civic life and effective citizens – certainly in higher education. But I worry that by leaning so heavily on a "problem" framework, we're actually compounding the... er...problem.

Problems, in our traditional understanding, are puzzles to be solved, or negative issues to be resolved. We might follow many paths to consider and contextualize those problems (insert list of all academic disciplines here). And we might apply many methods and means to address them (same list here). If we get fancy, we might combine multiple paths, methods, and means. But still, resolving the problem is the "end" and our paths and methods are the "means."

Artistic practice and process, on the other hand, proceed from a rather different understanding of a "problem." Often, in an artistic work, the "problem" is the work, itself: how to make a dramatic play "hold together," how to make a physical object "coherent," how to make a poem "whole." In artistic practice, the problem and solution evolve together, with a primary goal of finding the fulfillment of the creative work – not of resolving some external "problem." As H.W. Janson describes it in his *History of Art*:

> ...the creative process consists of a long series of leaps of the imagination and the artist's attempts to give them form by shaping the material accordingly. The hand tries to carry out the commands of the imagination and hopefully puts down a brush stroke, but the result may not be quite what had been expected, partly because all matter resists the human will, partly because the image in the artist's mind is constantly

> shifting and changing, so that the commands of the imagination cannot be very precise.... In this way, by a constant flow of impulses back and forth between his mind and the partly shaped material before him, he gradually defines more and more of the image, until at last all of it has been given visible form.[24]

The standard, dismissive response to this idea of an art work as its own problem would be "art for art's sake." To which I'm responding: *Yes, please.* Because so much of the power, insight, impact, and discovery derived through the arts come from this impulsion. As Michael Polanyi and Harry Prosch phrase it in *Meaning*:

> ...all the arts work in this way. They search for means of solving a problem – a problem which was conceived for this very purpose, i.e., its solution; and they pursue this question while continuing to shape the problem so that it will better fit the means for solving it.[25]

At the end of this exploration, if all goes well, is a coherent, compelling, even beautiful outcome – one that is problem, solution, question, and answer all at once.

Certainly, artistic process and practice have immeasurable value and opportunity "as tools" to explore, define, understand, and address complex problems around us. But a large part of that value comes from the different way they define and approach a "problem." While traditional problem formation is inevitably a reduction and partition, artistic problem formation is all about seeking and shaping a coherent whole. As E.M Forster argued back in 1949:

> Works of art, in my opinion, are the only objects in the material universe to possess internal order, and that is why, though I don't believe that only art matters, I do believe in Art for Art's Sake.[26]

Original blog post: June 7, 2017

15
NOTICING BEFORE KNOWING

"...what you notice depends on what you allow yourself to notice,
And that depends on what you feel authorized, permitted to notice
In a world where we're trained to disregard our perceptions."

VERLYN KLINKENBORG

My favorite books about writing are really books about thinking, and crafting those thoughts into powerful, public form. So, whenever I'm in a thinking thicket I look for insight in books about writing.

A frequent salvation in these moments is Verlyn Klinkenborg's *Several short sentences about writing*, an extended haiku of a book about clarity, intention, and rigor in the written word (and the thinking behind it). There are a thousand insights in the book, which I can't convey here (so read it). But what helps me immeasurably in my teaching and my own writing is his perspective on noticing, and the powerful forces that discourage or disallow us from noticing the world around us. Says Klinkenborg:

> Most people have been taught that what they notice doesn't matter,
> So they never learn how to notice,
> Not even what interests them.
> Or they assume that the world has been completely pre-noticed,
> Already sifted and sorted and categorized
> By everyone else, by people with real authority.
> And so they write about pre-authorized subjects in pre-authorized language.[27]

To address this challenge in my classroom, we spend a good amount of time learning to notice, and learning what it means to notice clearly and cleanly (being specific, withholding judgment, asking for evidence or detail if you hear what sounds like judgment: "what do you see that makes you say that?").

On occasion, we'll do this overtly by looking at a painting or short performance video together and working through the Critical Response Protocol developed and refined by the Perpich Center for Arts Education in Minnesota. In turn, I ask each student to share a detail, contrast, or technique that they notice in the painting or performance and describe it without judgment or conclusion. The process encourages the facilitator to repeat whatever is said, perhaps in different words, and to point to the item being noticed – which both validates the student's statement and focuses the attention of the other students on the detail. The process also highlights how individual attention can evolve into collective attention, particularly when judgment is delayed.

In another attempt at "attention boot camp," I assign each student an odd or innovative arts initiative to research and present to the class. The assignment directs them to share "things worth noticing" about the venture – what it does, how it does it, what's unique or different. Because the organizations selected are highly unusual in their mission or their methods, the other requirement is to share without judging – without positive or negative conclusions.

In another iteration, we all attended a free performance at major arts center. I assign a list of questions for each student to reflect upon and respond to – their first search for information about the event, their travel and approach to the venue, the performance itself, and their departure when it's over. At each phase, they are prompted to say what they noticed, rather than what they felt or concluded.

There's much to share about what students notice when encouraged to notice, and where it leads the conversation. But through it all, I notice how resonant Klinkenborg's conclusions are: That students have rarely been asked to notice, haven't been taught to notice in noncritical ways, and in some cases don't even known it's okay to notice for themselves.

Also resonant is the tendency toward "pre-authorized subjects in pre-authorized language," especially when talking about business structures and strategies. Students talk in business terms about business-like things already defined in their books and lectures. That's a useful part of knowing, but a stunted way of noticing.

Noticing seems to be a basic and obvious first step in building aesthetic attention, or in taking any thoughtful action in the world. But I am continually struck in my teaching how unnatural it has become for my students (and for me) to observe the details around us – clearly, cleanly, with attention and intent. When we do see something, it also seems unnatural not to judge it, or attach it immediately to some larger meaning. Again, Klinkenborg warns us about this tendency:

> What you notice has no meaning.
> Be sure to assign it none.
> It doesn't represent or symbolize
> Or belong to some world theory or allegory of perception.

I'm convinced that the road to mastery in cultural management (or many other things) is not about judging more quickly, but rather delaying judgment long enough to perceive clearly. Noticing seems to be the first, second, third, fourth, and fifth stop along the way. So, I will continue the search for and experiment with ways to build this capacity in my students and myself.

Original blog post: June 20, 2016

16

THE WORLD AND THE WHEELHOUSE

"I want to be famous in the way a pulley is famous, or a buttonhole, not because it did anything spectacular, but because it never forgot what it could do."

NAOMI SHIHAB NYE

When people say that an action, effort, or initiative is "in their wheelhouse" they tend to mean that it lies in the area of their greatest ability. The phrase seems to have become popular in baseball to mean "That part of the strike zone in which the batter swings with the most power or strength; the path of the batter's best swing."[28] Something to do with railroad roundhouses, or the place where a paddle-boat pilot works, or the like.

The phrase keeps coming to mind as we continue to discuss the value, impact, and expectations of public and nonprofit arts organizations, where I often find myself and my peers saying "should" a lot. Arts organizations *should* design and describe their public value. Arts organizations *should* serve a good beyond their own impulse to express. Arts organizations *should* serve diverse audiences and social issues and accessibility and excellence and on and on.

Pushback to this litany of shoulds often comes in the form of artistic freedom and creative emphasis: an arts organization's job is to foster exceptional voices and make extraordinary work. Aiming at other targets pulls focus, dilutes impact, and dulls vitality. And for many arts organizations, making exceptional creative work is in their wheelhouse (I'll let you define "exceptional" as it can legitimately mean many things). Swinging at a pitch above or below that zone feels awkward, doesn't connect, or pops up for an easy out.

But eventually it occurs to me that the art of an arts organization is not in the shoulds that pile on you, but in the coulds of connecting your work to the world. Could we focus our limited time, attention, and resources on the things we do best, and still make an impact beyond our circle? Could there be needs in the world that lie within the arc of our swing? Could we stretch just a little over time to increase that zone of possibility?

Author and philosopher Frederick Buechner wrote that "The place God calls you to is the place where your deep gladness and the world's deep hunger meet." Where do your wheelhouse and your world intersect? What could happen if you focused your energy there?

Original blog post: July 19, 2013

17

DISINTEREST, DISTANCE, AND THE ARTIST-MANAGER

"Studying a face
Stepping back to look at a face
Leaves a little space in the way like a window
But to see, it's the only way to see"
STEPHEN SONDHEIM

One of the core actions of aesthetic/artistic attention is to step back – to make a little space between yourself and the object of your attention, so you can see it as it is, rather than see it as you are. Stephen Sondheim captures this imperative (and its implications) in the song "Finishing the Hat," quoted above, from the musical *Sunday in the Park with George.*

In aesthetics, this approach or attitude is called "disinterest," not because you don't care about the work, but because you work to remove your immediate self from its observation. As one encyclopedia frames it: "The person who adopts the aesthetic attitude does not view (hear, taste, and so forth) objects with some kind of personal interest, that is, with a view to what that object can do for her, broadly speaking."[29] Instead, disinterest suspends your individual needs and goals to make space for observing the object or experience more fully.

English scholar Edward Bullough framed the same idea (back in 1912), but used the phrase "psychical distance" rather than disinterest. "Distance," he wrote, "is obtained by separating the object and its appeal from one's own self, by putting it out of gear with practical needs and ends."[30] Bullough suggested that a core strength and power for artistic expression and experience is this distance...we can observe intense events on a theater stage and know they're not real, but also be open to their emotional meaning and consequence.

Disinterest and distance don't mean "detachment," which Bullough makes clear: "Distance does not imply an impersonal, purely intellectually interested relation of such a kind. On the contrary, it describes a *personal* relation, often highly emotionally colored, but of a *peculiar character*" [emphasis from the original].

Why the aesthetics lesson? Because managers, particularly of cultural organizations, face a similar challenge. They can experience their charge according to their own emotions and needs, in which case they abandon the larger circles of people, purposes, and processes in play. Or, they can experience everything as distant, intellectual, and clinical, in which case they abandon the emotional and human aspects of the enterprise – approaching the organization as if it were a machine. Like Goldilocks, arts managers need to find the psychical distance that is "just right" for resilient and responsive management – not too close, not too far.

Bullough describes two extremes that limit aesthetic engagement: One is "under-distance," when the artist or observer connects too closely to the work and it becomes entirely about personal pleasure; the other is "over-distance," when the artist or observer is far afield, making the experience feel improbable, artificial, or empty.

In our quest to professionalize arts organizations and corporatize the selection, evaluation, and training of their managers, we've tended to drive toward over-distance. Professionals, we believe, behave in a disinterested way, they approach their job as systems engineers and process improvers. That said, we've also indulged our share of under-distanced leadership, where ego and individual whim are signifiers of excellence.

If we are to consider our management and organizational work with a more aesthetic eye, we'll need to include our own distance as part of the palette. We must learn to step back far enough to see, without ego, what's before us, but not so far that we lose our human and humane response.

Original blog post: June 19, 2017

18
ARE YOU THE PUPPET OR THE PUPPETEER?

Gonzo: "Who wants to watch dolls wiggle?
I mean, even I wouldn't do an act like that.
Doll wiggling?! Talk about boring." [exits]
Kermit: "I didn't have the heart to tell him."

THE MUPPET SHOW, SEASON 5, EPISODE 7

A reasonably long while ago, one of my master's students (thanks Syrah!) was writing her thesis on professional development, and she discovered and shared a theory on human cognitive development that keeps coming back to haunt me. While the name of the theory sounds clinical and detached, the concepts of Constructive-Developmental Theory are rather compelling.

At the heart of the theory, developed by Harvard professor Robert Kegan from the work of Jean Piaget, is the assumption that human development evolves from what we perceive and how we perceive our relation to it.

As one summary describes it:

> Kegan describes the orders of development in terms of what is "subject" and what is "object" at each order. Subjective beliefs are those that a person is embedded in, that is, taken for granted as true and cannot be called into question, and objective beliefs are those that can be reflected on and questioned. The process of development involves moving beliefs from the subjective realm to the objective realm.[31]

The reason this theory sticks with me is that it captures, quite well, my own experience of my development, and my experiences of others. But it also describes for me the various developmental stages of cultural managers. Some managers I meet clearly feel they are "subject to" their organization's structure and strategy, their work processes, their leadership style, their relationships to co-workers and superiors – they honestly can't separate these things from their immediate experience. Others, however, see these very same elements "as objects" for them to consider, take responsibility for, problem-solve around, and even change when the situation demands a different approach.

Over my academic and professional life, I can clearly recall moments when I suddenly started seeing a whole new sphere "as object" to consider and engage. I was pushed to these moments through frustration and confusion, or pulled to them by an author or teacher or colleague. I once thought, for example, that meaning in the performing arts was constructed on stage and delivered to the audience (the audience being "subject to" that transmission as recipients).

Then the work of John Dewey and others compelled me to consider meaning as co-constructed by both the artist and the audience, which meant my metaphors for managing that arts experience had to change. Later, I began to consider a larger system of co-constructed meaning, including not only the artist and the audience, but the staff, the board, the donors, and the wider community. And then, an idea that organizations and expressions were really interconnected, like some massive expressive energy grid.

None of this is to claim that I'm right in those assumptions, or those frames. But it seems a useful pursuit to increase the elements in ourselves and our environments we can perceive "as objects," to take responsibility for them, explore them, and problem-solve around them. That won't mean we can actually control our world, but at least we'll have a shot at living in it with more elegance, adaptability, and empathy.

Original blog post: January 18, 2013

PURPOSE & VALUE

19

THE FOOTPRINTS AND THE GIANT

Exploring the value of the arts to communities, a speech to the Rotary Club of Sheboygan, Wisconsin

Thank you for your invitation to speak to you today about the impact of the arts on communities. It's an essential topic any day, but particularly these days, as cities and counties come upon tight budgets and tough choices. And it's a subject that occupies a great deal of my work, for many reasons.

The title of my talk today is "The Footprints and the Giant," for reasons we'll soon explore together. But since all public speeches are supposed to begin with a joke, here's mine. Forgive me if you've heard it before, but there's a point to it:

> Sherlock Holmes and Doctor Watson are out in the woods on a camping trip. In the middle of the night, Sherlock Holmes shakes Doctor Watson awake and says to him, "Watson, look up at the sky and tell me what you deduce." So Watson rubs his eyes and looks up at the night sky, saying: "I see a billion stars, among

> which there may be a million planets, among which there may be planets much like our Earth, and upon which there may well be sentient life looking back at their night sky at this very moment, wondering if we might exist." After this speech, Sherlock Holmes pauses for a moment and responds, "No Watson, you idiot. Someone has stolen our tent."

The point of that particular joke for today's topic is this: Sometimes we work so hard to see the details in the distance that we completely miss the essential truth directly in front of us. I'm going to suggest that that's true when we explore the value of the arts to any of us and all of us. There are important details, to be sure, and we'll walk through them together. There are economic benefits, social benefits, educational or personal benefits, and broader civic benefits. These are important. They are compelling. And they are convincing when we ask individuals and groups to support the arts with time and money. But I'll also suggest that these arguments are really just the details in the distance I just mentioned in the joke. They are effects and not causes. They are the footprints a giant leaves behind, but they are not the giant. Today, we're going to talk a little about the giant, as well.

And, yes, I promise to do all this in the 15 to 20 minutes I've been provided to speak with you. While we'll likely argue about the value of the arts and how they should be supported, we all share a common value for our time. It's precious. And I won't waste too much of yours today.

But first a little background about me, so you know where I'm coming from. I'm the director of the MBA degree program in Arts Administration at the University of Wisconsin-Madison School of Business. It's a full-time, two-year degree program, now in its fourth decade, training future managers and leaders of primarily nonprofit and public cultural institutions – theaters, symphonies, festivals, performing arts centers, museums, public television and radio stations, foundations, government agencies, and such. Our graduates help bring arts experiences to small towns and big cities, here in Wisconsin, and across the country.

Now, I realize that to some people, combining "MBA" with "Arts" might seem as odd as combining "jumbo" with "shrimp." But you'll have to trust me that cultural institutions are businesses, they are complex puzzles, and they require a mastery of business strategy, financial skill, and social finesse that's often unrecognized. I'm sure that there are cultural managers and board members among you. Be sure to thank them, and thank yourselves, for doing the hard work required of this particular calling.

And as long as we're defining things, let me define what I mean by "the arts." It's a fuzzy word, often left undefined. Today, I mean to discuss the arts in broad strokes, as an inclusive concept. Certainly, I mean the traditional nonprofit arts we all could name, such as dance, classical music, theater, visual art, sculpture, and such. But I also mean community or amateur arts like the community choir, the embroidery club, the quilting bee, the amateur theater, the school art program, and the adult pottery classes. And I even mean the commercial side of the creative world – the nightclubs, the recording studios, the live performance venues and festivals, the commercial art galleries, the popular performers you might catch on tour in a local venue.

In short, "the arts" here mean any creative expression or experience available to you within your community – ticketed or free, formal or informal, professional or amateur, nonprofit or commercial, whether you watch it being made or you make it yourself. You can find these experiences in many places, but for today, I'm primarily talking about art that you experience in person, and not mediated through an electronic box like a television, a computer, or a radio. Not that these aren't important and meaningful. Just that I'm primarily talking about art in the community context.

So, given all that background, what is the value of the arts to communities? Why should we consider giving our money, our attention, our time, and even our tax dollars to be sure the arts are in our cities, our schools, and our civic life? Who cares if opportunities for creative expression and cultural experience are diverse, vital, and accessible to a full range of our fellow citizens?

Well, for one, a lot of people *do* care. They are the people that bring the arts to life: the artists, the volunteers, the audiences, the managers, the boards, the donors, the civic leaders. Ask most of these individuals and you'll hear that one art form or another has deep meaning for them, that it connects them, that it challenges them, that it calms them, that it reminds them of important people and moments in their lives, and that it brings them together with people and ideas they enjoy being with. There are many in the room that would say the arts are important because the arts are important *to them*...so important that they want other people to have that same experience, both now and in future generations.

But for the civic conversation, the praise of enthusiasts isn't quite enough. Some would say that it's great for people to find purpose and meaning in the arts, but not everyone does. Lots of people find purpose and meaning and even escape in fly fishing. But we don't allocate tax dollars or school district budgets for that. To expend community resources and attention, for any activity, we need reasonable assurance that the activity serves a public purpose...that it provides a public good.

This brings us to the broader arguments for the arts… the arguments that seek to show the wider public benefits of arts and culture, even to those who never attend. There are a lot of these arguments, but thankfully they come in four main flavors:[32]

Economic
Social
Educational or personal, and
Civic

Let's take them one at a time:

The *economic* arguments for the arts suggest that cultural activities bring economic benefits to a community. They draw audiences, who buy tickets for a show, but also dinner before and drinks afterwards. These audiences hire babysitters. They stay in hotels. Furthermore, in the process of attracting audiences, artists and arts organizations spend money, as well – on lumber and office equipment and staff. Some claim that the vitality and nightlife they bring to a region helps in stalking the elusive "knowledge worker," and the businesses that want to hire them. And arts organizations can be the anchors for downtown revitalization or development efforts, when those same knowledge workers are looking for a place to shop, to kick back, and to live.

The *social* arguments for the arts describe their power to gather people together, often across economic or cultural divides. While sociologists like Robert Putnam complain that American's are increasingly bowling alone, the arts are offered as an antidote to this isolation. They build trust and social capital. They reinforce the fabric that's often torn by the competitive marketplace. They foster empathy for different points of view and give a voice to individuals or groups that might be otherwise ignored.

The *educational and personal* arguments for the arts claim the learning or healing power of creative experience. Test scores improve. Creative thinking is enabled. Broken spirits and tired bodies are restored. Minds are refocused and refreshed.

The *civic* argument combines all of the above and suggests that a vibrant cultural life makes for a vibrant civic life – with high economic performance, high inward investment, high educational attainment, and high levels of civic engagement.

There's a great deal of discussion going on these days among advocates and academics about these benefits, about how we can measure them, and about how direct the connections might be between the arts and the outcomes we claim. The Wallace Foundation released a major study in February of this year, called *Gifts of the Muse*,[33] which explored each of these benefits, and the studies that supported them. The authors found that the arguments had merit, but that their connections were under-researched and often over-sold. Instead, the authors urged us all to focus less on what art does and more on what art is, and the intrinsic values it provides.

The topic of "valuing culture" pops up at almost every professional conference I attend these days. As government money gets tight, as personal fortunes took a hit in 2001 and beyond, and as discretionary spending got lean, arts advocates have been struggling for better arguments and clearer cases to ensure their programs and their missions. And as I've said, this conversation is important. There are hard choices ahead. City councils, county boards, state legislatures, and school boards are increasingly struggling with the math. Even the most eloquent arguments can't boost tax revenues or lower healthcare costs. Even the most convincing connections between arts and learning can't counter the constraints of revenue caps for public schools.

So, what arguments should we make, or can we make to ensure the vitality of creative experience and expression in our towns and cities? And what arguments can be heard, even, among the current climate of political gamesmanship?

Thankfully, even as we debate and craft our messages and strategies, artists and arts organizations quietly and effectively continue to find a way: they make art happen. While we struggle with semantics and public benefits, artists and arts organizations are gathering communities, forging new works, engaging young people, crafting new things to see and new ways to discover. Regardless of the arguments we attach after the fact, art is about what we do as a community, as individuals, as inhabitants of the same places here in Sheboygan, and in towns like Sheboygan across the country.

I'm sure you're all aware of many such active expressions of art in your own neighborhoods, among your businesses, and in your schools. You're fortunate to have an internationally recognized effort right here in town, in the Kohler Corporation's Arts/Industry program. This effort places working artists in residence in Kohler's manufacturing and design facilities, blending the company's ceramics and metalworking equipment and master craftspeople with visionary independent artists. Each learns from the other. Each pushes the other toward a new way of working and seeing. There are certainly benefits to this interaction, but they are outcomes not causes. The cause is the effort itself, the intensity of the conversation and challenge that creative visions provide, and the relationships such efforts bring.

Another example just happened in my hometown of Monona, just outside of Madison. My daughter is 11 years old, and her school just held an artist residency of its own. A wonderful performer, choir director, community member, and musician brought two middle schools from a common school district together to sing, to prepare for a public concert, and to work together toward that common goal. Again, there were benefits. The pride and supportiveness this event brought to the children was a wonder to behold. But again, these benefits were the effects, they were the impressions left by intense and creative effort among a group of people. These benefits were the outcomes, not the cause.

Which brings us back to the title of my talk with you today: "The Footprints and the Giant." The footprints are the impressions left by something very large, but they are not the thing, itself. Economic impact is a footprint. Social connection is a footprint. Education and personal growth are footprints. And a vital civic life is a footprint, as well. They are easier to talk about because they are the things we can see and measure. But like Doctor Watson straining to explain the night sky, our focus on the footprints can blind us to the more important point. The footprints get larger and deeper only if we understand the giant that leaves them.

Some might be asking what the heck I'm talking about. Others might be wondering when I will stop talking. For both groups, I'll cut to the chase: the giant that leaves these large impressions on our community is the process of creative expression and experience, itself. In the making of theater we discover each other and ourselves. In the interaction of artistic vision and personal perspective we make new connections. In striving to express who we are and what we see, we learn who we are and what we see. And through creative expression and experience, we have an astounding opportunity to share that effort and that vision with each other.

The arts are not a separate thing from us. They *are* us. The sculpture, the novel, the song, the painting, the performance, the musical work, the poem, the drawing, the photograph are all ways we see each other and ourselves. They are all ways of learning – ways that connect with so many students who have trouble connecting by traditional means. They are ways of reaching across perspectives and backgrounds. In fact, our collective expressions are often what define us long after we are gone. And they are how we know the people, places, and civilizations that came before us.

Art is us. All of us. And the massive secret that sits right in front of us is that *we* are the giant that leaves such wonderful footprints.

So, once more, back to the formal title of this talk: what is the "impact of the arts," and the "benefit of culture to communities"? The glaring truth is that art *is* community. It is the reflection and expression of what we all do, what we all are, and what we all hope to be.

So, while we're striving to describe the footprints, I encourage us all to focus the bulk of our energies on the giant, before we, like Sherlock Holmes and Doctor Watson, wake up to realize that someone has stolen our tent.

This speech was originally prepared for and delivered to the Rotary Club of Sheboygan, Wisconsin, May 23, 2005, when I was serving as faculty and director for the Bolz Center for Arts Administration at the University of Wisconsin-Madison. The speech was also published in Logue, Cal M., Lynn Messina, and Jean Laura DeHart, eds. Representative American Speeches, 2005-2006. *New York: H.W. Wilson, 2006.*

20
PUBLIC, PRIVATE, PLURAL

"...the plural sector comprises all associations of people that are owned neither by the state nor by private investors."

HENRY MINTZBERG

In the U.S. we've agreed to disagree about what to call that "other" sector of collective action that isn't private (aka, privately owned business) and isn't public (aka, government). Non-profit, not-for-profit, third, social, civil, voluntary all capture bits of it, but miss important bits as well. Which is why I'm increasingly fond of Henry Mintzberg's framing and naming for this other sector: plural.

In *Rebalancing Society*, Mintzberg suggests "plural" as the best way to consider the intentions, actions, and purposes for this other sector. And he further suggests that vibrant societies are about balance rather than single-sector strength. Says he:

> Strength in all three sectors is necessary for a society to be balanced. Imagine them as the sturdy legs of a stool – or pillars, if you wish – on which a healthy society has to be supported: a public sector of politi-

> cal forces rooted in respected governments, a private sector of economic forces based on responsible businesses, and a plural sector of social forces manifested in robust communities.[34]

Mintzberg is certainly not the first to suggest a three-legged platform for thriving societies. But his framing of "plural" as one of those legs is a productive contribution because it includes a vast range of collective efforts – not just formal institutions – such as social movements, cooperatives, and informal collaborations.

Of course, formal institutions are still in there too: not-for-profit arts organizations, educational institutions, social services, volunteer enterprises. But they are surrounded by the dark matter of millions of informal and often unrecognized collectives that support and advance a resilient plural life.

Mintzberg is also clear that each of the three sectors has unique strengths, but also insidious downsides – private (markets) can be crass, public (governments) can be crude, plural (communities) can be closed – which is why each sector must strive toward its best self and learn to play well with others.

The plural sector is *not* a midpoint between private and public. It is a third way of attracting, aligning, and activating people and resources. It's a framing and naming that's worth a ride around the block.

Original blog post: August 10, 2018

21
SHOCK AND "EH"

"My name is Ozymandias, King of Kings;
Look on my Works, ye Mighty, and despair!"
PERCY BYSSHE SHELLEY

I've been to enough "creative economy" presentations to know how they generally flow: They draw a big circle and then flash a big number. The big circle includes lots of creative industries – from nonprofit to full-on-profit. The big number comes from their aggregated economic activity. The message is, essentially: Holy cow, we're big. Therefore, we're important. Pay attention. Make nice with us.

For example, Americans for the Arts points to $135.2 billion of economic activity. The Orange Economy flags the sector as worth 6.1 percent of the world economy (quoting John Howkins). The NEA and the US Department of Commerce sets "arts and cultural production" in the US as 4.32 percent of the Gross Domestic Product – more than construction, more than transportation and warehousing.

But while the big circle/big number approach does offer a first-blush flourish, it tends to dissipate rather quickly, without leaving much behind. Because, yes, the creative economy is big, but it's also diffuse. And while the former is animating and validating, the latter is a bit of a problem.

For an allegory, consider the penny: There are approximately 200 billion pennies currently in circulation. That's $2 billion in economic value, with serious collective weight, size, and significance (stacked together, they'd form two cubes at 127 feet per side). By the "big number" playbook, that makes pennies a big deal, worthy of attention, praise, and preferential policy.

But just try to use your 127-foot cube of pennies to buy a single can of soda from a vending machine or add time to your parking meter to avoid a ticket. Those systems don't work with just aggregated wealth, they require concentrated wealth (nickels, dimes, and quarters). The pennies may have comparable value, but they don't have comparable utility. Which is why you likely have a jar of them sitting in your closet.

The same challenges face the creative industries. Even if they generate more economic value than the hotel industry, the hotel industry has bigger players with more concentrated wealth. Which makes them more coordinated and consequential in the policy machine. That doesn't mean, necessarily, that policy makers are focused on fat-cats. It just means it's easier to attend to concentrated wealth than a million little bits of wealth scattered here and there. Coordinated advocacy helps a lot, of course, but you're still advocating for pennies in a world that prefers quarters.

I'm not saying we should avoid the "big number" flourish, or the big-tent perspective on creative industries. I'm just saying that we should never consider the big circle/big number pitch a persuasive argument.

It's not an argument. It's an opener. And most of the creative economy presentations I've seen misunderstand the complexity of the close.

Original blog post: June 9, 2016

22

WHAT THE WEALTH WANTS

"S/he who pays the piper calls the tune."

THE WEALTH (although not always out loud)

I focus a fair amount of my research and reading time on the issues of capital structure and infrastructure investment in the nonprofit arts (exciting, I know). I'm intrigued by whether and how arts organizations build, buy, or borrow infrastructure (buildings, technology, staffing infrastructure, professional development). And why they so often seem to end up with structures that are too complex or cumbersome to sustain without significant corporate calisthenics and mission drift. And I'm finding that – regardless of sector, tax status, industry, or organization size – the answer is captured in a rather simple question:

What does the wealth want?

"Wealth," here means any source of significant resources required for an organization to do its work. Wealth can be held by an individual (in the form of a private owner of a for-profit company, or an individual philanthropist). It can be held by an organizational aggregation of resources (a foundation, an investment company, a bank). It can be held by a public agency (where wealth is the aggregate tax income and service fees collected by a city, county, state, or nation). Or it can be held by a "marketplace" of those individuals, organizations, or agencies – where no one player holds dominant resources, but where the market, itself, has behaviors you can track over time.

Any of these holders of wealth can make choices about where to direct their wealth. Some holders are constrained in those choices (nonprofit foundations, for example, are generally limited to tax-exempt organizations). But even within those constraints, they can choose. They make those choices rationally or non-rationally, through evidence or impulse, through publicly stated objective or hidden but emergent patterns. And the organizations and individuals seeking that wealth adjust their behavior and position accordingly – either consciously or unconsciously.

Privately held for-profit companies are initially defined by the desires of their owners. If they seek bank loans or angel investors, they become subject to the wants and needs of that wealth. Publicly traded companies are defined by the collective wants and needs of their stockholders – sometimes concentrated in a few large players, sometimes diffused among a crowd.

So what wealth drives the behavior of nonprofit arts organizations? And what does that wealth want? Obviously, the mix and the matrix are different for every organization. Some are dependent on a few large donors. Some are supported by many small gifts. Some are bending toward organized philanthropy. Some are defined and designed by the people who contribute their time and talents (which are also essential forms of wealth).

Sometimes, this influence is not from a market or a matrix, but from an individual. We've all been in board meetings where the largest donor at the table takes or is given the dominant weighting in board decisions (a variation on the dreaded and distorting HiPPO, or "Highest Paid Person's Opinion" in business meetings). It's one of the primary challenges of conflating governance and fundraising, giving "the wealth" the keys to the nonprofit kingdom.

Of course, there's no crime or credit in any particular funding bundle. Just a need to understand how your current resources, and any desired new resources, might influence your choices about investing, acting, reflecting, or connecting in the world.

If you and your mission want the same thing that the wealth wants, good on you! If you don't want the same thing, or if your mission or community demand a different path than what the wealth wants, be prepared to align those wants or leave the money on the table and walk away.

Original blog post: July 29, 2013

23
INVOCATION AND ALLOCATION

"O for a Muse of fire..."
WILLIAM SHAKESPEARE

Since the universe for arts and cultural enterprise is ever-evolving, and since I happen to teach in a master's degree program that claims to prepare high-performing leaders for that universe, I spend an unreasonable amount of time trying to define what I do for a living, and how I do it. That effort is a key engine behind my writing, which helps me frame and float ideas for all of you to refute or refine.

In the process of defining what I do for a living, I'm continually drawn back to the quote attributed to Albert Einstein, that the best models are "as simple as can be, but not simpler."[35]

So what is the simplest (but not over-simplified) way to describe what a master's in Arts Management does, or can do? What might define and refine what my colleagues and I do every day? Here's what I've got at the moment:

> "We foster a more elegant invocation and allocation of people, time, stuff, and money toward expressive ends."

There's a lot to unbundle in that sentence, so perhaps I haven't hit Einstein's mark just yet. But two words that keep evolving for me will be my focus here: invocation and allocation.

"Invocation" includes any activity that draws resources toward an artistic or expressive effort – talented artists, craftspeople, and technicians; staff and support personnel; board members and volunteers; audiences; earned and contributed income; space and equipment and raw materials. "Invocation" arose as the best word, because all of these resources are truly about summoning energy toward you, calling for aid and insight and inspiration. That's an invocation.

"Allocation" includes anything you do to align, assign, direct, constrain, or evaluate how those resources are applied toward the expressive end. This involves, often, control and analysis functions like accounting and finance, but also a full range of strategic efforts toward what my colleague Russell Willis Taylor calls "doing less better."

These two bundles of effort require different skills and abilities, and often live in tension with each other. So, the other thing that "elegance" requires is continual balance and care.

It might be shocking to some that the word "creation" isn't anywhere in my summary sentence. But to be honest, I don't prepare people to create artistic works. My graduates support, advance, sustain, connect, commission, encourage, and refine creative works toward their successful expression and stewardship. Creative and expressive work is the center and purpose of all that they do. But the work they do is primarily invocation, allocation, and the dance between the two.

Original blog post: August 16, 2011

24

OWNERSHIP, WITHOUT THE AIR QUOTES

Many may be aware, and some may be annoyed, that I wrestle a lot with the concepts of "capital" – what it is, how it works, and what it does in the context of the nonprofit arts. The issue draws my focus for three broad reasons. First, it's a big, recurring, juicy issue for arts boards, leaders, funders, and policy makers. Second, those same people seem to lack a useful frame and language for engaging the issue productively. And third, the lens and language we've borrowed from the commercial world are often more elusive than illuminating.

Capital is any aggregated resource available for or applied to the generation of more resources. As architect Bill McDonough phrased it: "capital is currency with potential."[36] Capital comes in two broad types, which we often conflate: "financial capital" includes the money, credit, and other forms of funding required to make stuff or provide services that generate revenue; "capital goods" include physical structures, equipment, and objects required to make stuff or provide services that generate revenue.

You can recognize capital when you see it because it is durable over multiple years or business cycles (think factory or endowment); it is required for the production of a product or outcome but doesn't become part of the product or outcome (think table saw or hair clippers); nor is capital significantly transformed by the production process (except for wear and tear, which we acknowledge through depreciation).

That's a lot for a few paragraphs. Sorry.

No matter which way you wander to discover "capital," you run into a wall called "ownership." In much of the available research, the two concepts of capital and ownership are so deeply intertwined that they are almost codependent. Durable resources are aggregated, applied, and evaluated by an owner, or by an entire marketplace of owners observing each others' successes and mistakes. Resources find their best use in comparison to all other possible uses by those who control them, and through the lens of optimal return (of money, of mission, of public good).

When we talk about capital among nonprofits, however, we rarely acknowledge that ownership is fundamentally different. If you don't recall how it's different, here are some short and sloppy bullet points to remind you:

> In the *private* sector, assets are owned by *somebody*;
> In the *public* sector, assets are owned by *everybody*;
> In the *nonprofit* sector, assets are owned by *nobody*, but rather held in trust.

And yet we talk about "capital" in each of these sectors in strikingly similar terms.

In *The Ownership of Enterprise*, Henry Hansmann defines "owners" as "those persons who share two formal rights: the right to control the firm and the right to appropriate the firm's profits, or residual earnings..."[37] The word "formal" is important, since often an individual with a formal right to control has no effective means of control (a minority stockholder, for example, can't control very much other than their inconsequential vote for corporate board members, or their inconsequential vote for merger or dissolution). But still, owners have rights (whether or not they can execute them). They have the larger right to enter or exit their ownership status in response to their assessment of its worth. And they feel the consequence, rather viscerally, if they choose well or poorly.

Yet, for a sector without any formal owners, the nonprofit arts talk about "ownership" a lot (consider those quotation marks to be air quotes). Or, rather, we talk about building a "sense of ownership" – a phrase that's like air quotes, but with most of the air let out. The difference between "ownership" and a "sense of ownership" is like the difference between "danger" and a "sense of danger." One has serious and immediate consequence. The other offers narrative value, and an occasional nudge to behavior.

When I share this point with my successful practitioner colleagues, several have said it's a matter of semantics rather than deep concern. Boards essentially act as the owner, they say, even though the board members don't always know whose interests they represent, and don't feel direct consequence for bad decisions. They also say that good boards know to drive resources, impact, and leadership – which is most of their job. And that good executives can navigate them over the tricky bits. But I think the problem is beyond such jerry-rigging.

I've written before (and others have argued better than me) about the missing value of equity investment in the nonprofit arts (not better than other values, but a useful one in certain circumstances). I've also written about the unique challenge of closing a nonprofit, when there are no owner incentives or consequences to inform the difficult choice. But now I'm wondering more broadly about ownership, and the dynamics that come from removing ownership from control – both contractually and effectively.

And again (as ever), I'm not calling for ownership in the nonprofit arts. I'm just exploring the unique challenges of governing, managing, and supporting an ownerless enterprise. That's what nonprofit arts leaders do, after all. So we might as well know, with some clarity and conviction, what that work entails.

Original blog post: May 28, 2014

25
CREATIVE, EXPRESSIVE, CONNECTED, REMEMBERED

"Cultural policy is society's mechanism for shaping expressive life. It is the framework of law, regulation, and customary behavior in which art, information, and knowledge are created, distributed, consumed, and preserved."

BILL IVEY

At almost every arts advocacy event, I am struck by the loss of words we suffer when arguing for public expenditure for arts and culture. Economic impact is still limping along as an angle for some. Creative economy arguments seem to be strong but peaking. Tourism and education are also contenders for talking points. And, of course, an effective advocacy strategy blends all of the above in response to its audience.

For me, four phrases bubble up from the speeches, presentations, and conversations at advocacy events. It seems to me that a diverse, rich, and vital cultural ecology in any city, state, or country fosters opportunity for every citizen to inform these elements of their existence:

A Creative Life
The opportunity to make something from nothing, or transform fragments of objects or thoughts into a cohesive whole, is an ennobling and empowering thing. Everyone should have the option to do so, no matter what their stage of life, circumstance, technical ability, or training.

An Expressive Life
Finding your voice and having an opportunity to be heard is an essential quality of being alive and aware in the world.

A Connected Life
The interpersonal and social sharing of meaning is the connective tissue between loved ones, community members, and civilizations. While the arts are not the only means to this sharing, they are among the most powerful and enduring.

A Remembered Life
The accumulated actions and artifacts of our expressive lives are our most vital threads to who we were, who we are, and who we might become. Beyond our children, they are the most compelling evidence that we ever existed at all.

While these four elements, combined, may influence positive external effects for a city, a county, a state, or a country, they carry the most power when fostered as a central focus of public policy, rather than as tools toward other goals. Perhaps I'm naive to suggest such intrinsic goals for cultural policy and public subsidy. But I keep noticing that we get lost in the arguments we've constructed, and forget the reasons we exist.

Original blog post: March 19, 2007

26
MEASURING ONLY WHEN WE MEAN IT

"Inchworm, inchworm
Measuring the marigolds
Seems to me you'd stop and see
How beautiful they are"
FRANK LOESSER

There are all sorts of interesting things about Netflix, and their ongoing incursion into program development in addition to content delivery. The company that used to mail you DVDs (and killed Blockbuster Video in the process) transitioned into a production company (making television studios anxious in the process).

But what caught my attention in this transition was their strategy for measuring success. Internally, they define and observe metrics about "engagement" with their content (which seem to track frequency, duration, and loyalty). Externally, they don't breathe a word about what they've found.

As Netflix rose to become a producing company, reporter after reporter grilled Chief Content Officer Ted

Sarandos for the numbers. Invariably, he declined. In fact, he didn't even share the metrics with the actors and creative teams who make the shows.

Why not share the numbers, especially if they claim they're outstanding? Because there's no value to Netflix in sharing the numbers out loud. They don't sell advertising, so ratings don't draw advertising money. They don't sell content to cable or media distributors, so ratings aren't necessary to confirm licensing value. They don't need numbers to convince viewers to watch. And since they make full-season or multi-season commitments to the creative team, they don't need to share numbers to signal shows in danger of cancellation.

Further, they seem to recognize that a new kind of programming model could only be damaged or distracted by an old kind of measurement.

Here's why that strategy is particularly interesting to me:

In my wanderings, I've been to a *lot* of arts conversations, and read a lot online, about measurement and evaluation, particularly around "impact." The "how" of measuring an organization's impact is fascinating and essential. We all need new tools to explore what we do, and explain how we change the world around us. But the "why" and "when" of impact measurement has often felt squishy.

As a start, let's imagine a world where you only measure something because that measurement matters to you, because it makes a difference to know it. Further, that measurement might matter for two reasons. One, you and your team care about informed internal decisions – you really care about outcomes and want to be sure you're continually investing your time, attention, and resources in the best possible way to get there. That's why Netflix is designing and monitoring "engagement" related to their new productions. Two, you measure something because those metrics will attract specific external resources – audiences will be encouraged to attend because they know something is well attended, funders will provide and continue support on the expectation of certain impact, governments and citizens will invest in something that demonstrates outcomes they value.

I say *specific* external resources, because convincing other people to select and favor you over other options is not a generic game. If a specific funder seeks specific evidence of your impact or success, you have reason to measure exactly that thing. If a partner organization is committed to social or civic or educational or personal impact, then again, you might consider developing impact metrics to prove your worth to that partner. If quotes or testimonials convince potential audiences to attend, then by all means gather quotes and testimonials.

In contrast, so much of the impact measurement conversation I've experienced feels like prospecting. We're aware, generically, that some funding sources might want feedback about our work and its impact or outcomes. We assume that if we increase our impact evaluation, that money will flow toward us. But in the meanwhile, we can diffuse our energies and distract our boards in these generic pursuits to make generic points.

If you care internally about good decisions, and metrics will help you (and they will, if they're specific), then measure. If you are specifically aware of external value that will flow your way if you can express your impact in specific ways, then measure. If neither of these is true, then really, don't bother. Measuring won't make a measurable difference.

Original blog post: March 7, 2013

27
CONTRACTS AND COALITIONS

"...most organizations are simply legal fictions which serve as a nexus for a set of contracting relationships among individuals."

MICHAEL C. JENSEN & WILLIAM H. MECKLING

We talk a lot in the arts about "organizations" – their missions, their purpose, their operations, their business models, their relationships with communities and constituents. Organizations have boards that oversee them, and executives who operate them. It's rather easy to think about an organization as a "thing" or a material being (dare I say "corporeal being," since it comes from a related root to "corporation"?). And, of course, the United States Supreme Court has thought this way more than once.

But if your job or your passion requires you to create, manage, or lead an organization, an overly simple definition of the thing doesn't help you much. It would be like building or maintaining a facility with no specific insight on what that facility was or did – courthouse, adobe hut, nuclear power plant, fast-food restaurant, or minivan.

Two related but distinct "theories of the firm" (which is what we call such theories of organization) help me to engage the question. One is economic. One is behavioral. Both attempt to describe what it is, exactly, we're managing when we manage an organization.

A useful economic theory of the firm defines an organization as a "nexus of contracts"[38] – a solution to market and coordination problems that occur when creating complex goods and services. Instead of hundreds of independent, temporary, individual agreements between producers, suppliers, owners, operators, and coordinators, an organization creates a single mooring to tie many contracts to the same pier.

When it's cheaper/easier to get something done within that mooring, you create "internal" contracts (through hiring staff, purchasing buildings or equipment, and so on). When it's cheaper/easier to get something done on the open market, you create "external" contracts (through freelancers or consultants, leasing rather than purchase, and so on). To facilitate these choices, our legal systems have given independent rights to organizations to make such contracts. While organizations/corporations aren't people, they have legal rights to do some of the things that people can do.

More recent scholarly work suggests that the internal/external distinction isn't particularly useful or true (for example, the "purchase/lease" distinction becomes pretty squishy when the lease is for decades). So, instead of thinking of an organization as a clear, hard shell around a bundle of contracts, it can be better to think of it as a hazy nexus or network of contracts, some of which are explicit (written and signed) and some of which are implicit (mutually understood or forged through tradition). There's a dense center bundle and a looser surrounding bundle, but the boundary between them is fuzzy and gray.

While *economic* theories tend to explore markets and pricing mechanisms (where people and firms are "rational actors" seeking to maximize gain), *behavioral* theories focus on observed human behavior (suggesting that neither people nor firms are primarily rational, nor do they know what they're maximizing).

One behavioral theory of the firm, therefore, suggests that organizations are always coalitions of individuals, and that those individuals have complex, changing, and often unrecognized motives. Contracts (or explicit agreements) are one way of aligning or directing these individuals, but they are insufficient. Even the profit motive isn't as magical as we think it is in aligning behavior. As Richard Cyert and James March put it in their foundational book *A Behavioral Theory of the Firm*:

> We can argue that entrepreneurs, like anyone else, have a host of personal motives. Profit is one, perhaps, but they are also interested in sex, food, and saving souls.[39]

As we know from observing government and our own networks, coalitions are formed by aligning intent and purpose, or through side-dealing, manipulation, and coercion when other means aren't working (I'm looking at you, *Game of Thrones*). While contracts often carry defined descriptions and durations, coalitions are shifting and organic things requiring constant care and conversation. Coalitions also cross organizational and sector boundaries, including partners and affiliates and supporters and advocates and funders and others. And coalitions don't have "centers" as much as they have "nodes" or multiple anchors, each with its own complex network.

So, to consider an organization as a stable "thing" that can have a vision and mission, that you are employed by, and that exists as some material entity is not just a legal fiction, it's a delusion. The more useful question for managers is whether they are managing a nexus of contracts or an amorphous and continually changing coalition defined by power, passion, politics, and individual preferences.

To which the answer is: Yes, exactly.

Original blog post: August 15, 2014

28

BELONGING GONE BAD

"...at the heart of sectarianism are distorted expressions of positive human needs for identity and belonging."
JOSEPH LIECHTY & CECELIA CLEGG

The idea of "belonging" has long been a key point of aspiration and advocacy for the arts. Art builds empathy. Art builds community. Art infuses a sense of belonging into a world so desperate for it. In these conversations, the problem is framed as a "lack of belonging," and arts experiences are the solution. But history and human behavior suggest a more complex truth.

While we tend to consider "belonging" a universally positive force, even a cursory glance at human history shows violence and injustice fueled by intense feelings of belonging – an entrenched "us and them" dynamic that makes the "them" demonic, inhuman, or one-dimensional.

A compelling conversation between Irish poet/author/community-leader Pádraig Ó Tuama and host Krista Tippett[40] explores the idea that "belonging" can both create and destroy communities. Ó Tuama calls the destructive aspect "belonging gone bad."

The focus of their conversation is the conflict around Northern Ireland over most of the 20th century, and its slow reconciliation. But the themes have universal significance and particular importance to present-day efforts in the arts.

The book Ó Tuama mentions as a source for "belonging gone bad" is *Moving Beyond Sectarianism* by Joseph Liechty and Cecelia Clegg, a thorough and even-handed exploration of North Ireland's dark history.[41] The authors describe sectarianism as a system fueled by entrenched feelings of group belonging, a deadly mix of religion and politics, where the "other" is demonized and discounted as inhuman.

Despite the destructive force of sectarianism, the authors argue that at its heart "are distorted expressions of positive human needs for identity and belonging." They go one step further to describe how those who reject sectarianism can actually reinforce it by following a similarly destructive pattern of thought: "encounter - judge - condemn - reject - demonize - separation/antagonism."

How do you know the difference between "right belonging" and "wrong belonging"? Liechty and Clegg suggest untangling the connections between intentions and consequences, since all sides can usually claim good intentions. "If the outcome entails the development of, or the augmenting of, one or more destructive patterns of relating, then the speech or action can be judged to be sectarian," they write.

As naturalist Aldo Leopold phrased the same idea in a different context: "A thing is right when it tends to preserve the integrity, stability, and beauty of the biotic community. It is wrong when it tends otherwise."[42]

Belonging is certainly at the core of so many conflicts among us. Much of it springs from the "dis-belonging" that hides beneath our community-building initiatives. Much of it festers in forms of belonging that starve and separate our humanity rather than feeding and connecting it.

Artistic expression and experience have a powerful role to play. But that role must be informed by a deep and clear-eyed view of the world – one without platitudes or generalizations about "belonging." The greatest artists and arts experiences can see and share this way. Arts organizations, administrators, and supporters should strive toward the same eyes-and-arms-wide-open objective.

Original blog post: June 1, 2017

29
SOVEREIGNTY OR SERVICE

"...when I feel most lost in this world, I comfort myself by visiting a hardware store...A hammer is still my Jesus, and my Virgin Mary is still a cross-cut saw."
KURT VONNEGUT

We often talk about an organization having a mission, as if the organization exists as some separate entity with its own individual will. But increasingly I'm wondering if that attribution hasn't always been upside-down. Organizations don't have missions. Missions have organizations. And when change is necessary, it's important to know which changes which.

Of course, organizations in the legal sense are often entities separate from their owners, managers, or staff. Long ago, civil society decided to make them separate, and give them some of the rights of individuals – to be party to a contract, to establish ownership or obligation for the entity rather than for its parts. But this was always a legal and economic fiction, not a natural fact.

Somewhere along the way, we started stretching this fiction to consider the organization as some sort of collective organism. And we started talking about the organization having a mission, constructed and confirmed over time by its constituent parts. The mission could be changed, even as the organization remained much the same. Because the organization determined its mission, not the other way around.

But underneath it all, an organization is *not* a separate, sentient entity that can choose its purpose. It is a tool, a resource, a means by which people get things done. An organization is not an organism, it is a crosscut saw, made useful by its structure and design for a particular range of outcomes. When the crosscut saw no longer fits the task, it doesn't redefine the carpenter or the blueprint, rather the carpenter reaches for a different tool.

Perhaps it's all semantics, but here's the larger point: When we consider the organization as a primary, sovereign self, our work inevitably turns toward ensuring its success, survival, and sovereignty. But the organization is not sovereign, nor is it a self. It's a hand tool in service to a larger purpose. Let's not be so precious, or so self-important, about changing it up or switching it out.

Original blog post: October 12, 2017

30
UTILITY VS. MORTALITY

"While aeons brush us with unheeded wing,
We hoard our little minutes one by one."
JANET NORRIS BANGS

How do you spend and save your money each day, within the context of your whole life? It sounds like a philosophical question, but it's actually a rather essential economics question. And as with most economics questions, it has a really cool and convoluted name: intertemporal consumption.

Intertemporal consumption explores the way we spend money from our past, present, or future. When you spend your savings, you're spending money from your past (accumulated income, among other things). When you spend your current income, you're spending from your present (earned now, spent now). When you save or borrow, you're shifting your consumption to or from the future (saving to spend it later, or borrowing to spend future income now).

The old-school economic answer to the question is that we humans, as rational actors seeking to maximize our own utility, divide our entire life's earnings into equal parts, which we spend each year (like an annuity). Because we earn less when we're younger, that means we would borrow more early on to support that rate. And, as we earn more, we borrow less and less, until our income exceeds our annuity rate and we then begin to save the surplus. Then as income declines post-retirement, we'd spend the balance.

While this all sounds entirely rational, and utility maximizing, it turns out it doesn't test well against actual human behavior.

Behavioral economists have a different theory, suggesting that we have three independent accounts in our heads from which we spend with different propensities: current income (which we spend easily), current assets (which we spend less easily), and future income (which we don't spend easily at all). This tests better.

Why does this matter to arts and cultural managers? I thought you'd never ask.

This matters in lots of ways. The theories have obvious impact on how we consider philanthropy (both our own, and those of our prospective donors). They also have impact on how we encourage different age segments in our audiences to spend on us. But what intrigues me most is how intertemporal consumption theory relates to how we decide to spend anything over our lifetimes – money, time, attention, energy – all of it in finite supply, all of it spread over decades, and all of it subject to momentary judgment each moment of our day.

So, what do we spend on action, what on reflection, what on sacred or silent time? And how does this grand calculus fit into our decisions about engagement with culture and creative expression?

Each of us makes choices every day to spend or save the resources we have accrued, or think we'll accrue, across all the days we have. An arts organization, and therefore an arts manager, is both a steward and a solicitor of intertemporal consumption.

Original blog post: May 2, 2013

31
IF CULTURE COUNTS, HOW DO WE COUNT IT?

Keynote address to the CAPACOA Conference: "Culture Counts: Measuring the Value of the Arts"

This convening focuses on how to measure what we value. So, I thought I should begin by defining what I value in professional convenings like this. We are all here for a few days (I mean here at this conference, not here on earth). And while many of us attend many such convenings, the opportunities they provide are extremely rare.

Certainly, many of you communicate on-line and by phone, as fellow professionals in a common industry. You happen upon each other at community galas or opening nights. But here we are, all together, all focusing on a common theme. It's easy to forget how extraordinary this is.

This is what performance analysts in the corporate world call "face time" – real people in real space in real time. And you might be shocked by the energy spent, especially in large corporations, optimizing "face time" for their salespeople, their support staff, and their chief executives (sometimes to encourage more, sometimes to urge less).

Many of us in this room are also in the business of "face time." Audiences, artists, donors, trustees, and volunteers commit this rare resource into our care. It's an awesome responsibility, and a glorious gift. We'll get to that soon.

Such convenings, therefore, deserve respect and clarity. In deference to both, I'll express out loud what I value in these rare moments:

Discourse

Face-to-face, we have an extraordinarily rich communication opportunity. I see you, you see me. There's content, of course, but the context surrounding it is rich and full of meaning and nuance. In technology terms, this is very high bandwidth. We can forge meaning and understanding here better than anywhere. We should make every opportunity to talk back and forth.

Discovery

With so much knowledge, experience, and perspective in one place, at the bandwidth I just described, there's an astounding opportunity for discovery – finding a new way of saying something we implicitly knew but couldn't express; hearing an angular view of something we only saw in one dimension; listening to what one of my colleagues calls our "inner conference" – that interior dialogue that's running within each of us right now, triggered by the conversations around us, perhaps, but running independently. It's a powerful part of how conferences work, and I encourage you to honor both the outer and inner conferences now underway.

Connection

You all are part of a densely connected network, which has gained in power and intensity through the on-line world. But there's even more power in having pieces of that network together in space and time. You can hear about a project or concern of a colleague, and instantly connect them to another colleague that is on a similar path – not just with an e-mail, but in person. It's like "speed dating" for the isolated arts warrior in all of us. High touch. High bandwidth. High context.

Finally, to take full advantage of the opportunities above, I also suggest a fourth element that makes all of them more likely and more profound:

Boldness & Humility

All productive conversations I've experienced balance the values of boldness and humility: Boldness to say out loud what you believe to be true, or to express honestly what you don't understand; humility to accept that you are likely wrong, as all of us are, if not in fact then by degree. This delicate dialectic is crushed by posturing and politics. I hope we make space for it here.

I'm sure you have other things you value about these convenings. And I encourage you to voice them to your inner conference as we progress. But let's begin with these. Plus, I'm the one with the microphone, so I get to pick for now.

Discourse, discovery, connection, boldness, humility. I say these things out loud so you can hold me accountable, and so that you can help me stay true to what I claim to be important. You're all smart enough to know when someone states a core value and then violates it with their actions. Heaven knows your audiences and communities are smart enough, too. When you call a customer service center, for example, and a recorded message tells you how much they value your call, you know they don't value your call quite enough to answer it.[43] When a speaker says they value discourse and then continues with a monologue, you know that their wires are crossed. In fact, if I'm still talking at 10:25, someone in the back should waive at me. That will be an indicator to me that I'm not serving the things I value. I want to leave time to talk together.

Beyond someone waiving at 10:25, I'll need some other indicators to help me define what I value with increasing clarity and determine if my actions actually serve what I say I value. And, since I'm a busy person who is easily distracted, my indicators need to have a few basic qualities: they should be *spontaneously generated*, *easily observable*, and *reasonably connected* to the value I have in mind. In a perfect world, my indicators should also be *participatory*, so other people can carry some of the burden and have an active voice in the process.

Let's explore those requirements, one-by-one:

> *Spontaneously generated*
> That is, not generated by me, but by the natural progression of the world, the residue of action or activity.
>
> *Easily observable*
> As I said, I'm busy and easily distracted, if an indicator is overly complex to extract or observe, I won't use it.
>
> *Reasonably connected*
> If I can't readily explain how the indicator is relevant to my stated values, it's probably time to find another.
>
> *Participatory*
> If indicators are available and obvious to a distributed group of people – especially those who have a stake in the value at work – I can have a bunch of eyes watching on my behalf, and again, keeping me honest. My eyes are biased, after all, as are all of our individual views of the world.

What might those indicators look like? Here's a first shot that I'll be using today. If I deliver a keynote consistent with my stated values:

> At least one of you will publicly disagree with me (respectfully, of course).

> At least three of you will feel compelled to send me a related link or resource that you connected to some element of my speech (tell me directly, hand me a note, send me an e-mail, post a comment to my weblog, whatever).
>
> At least two panelists or speakers will echo a phrase or concept from my conversation, or your response, over the course of this event – again, either agreeing with it, or disagreeing…don't care which.
>
> I will change my mind on at least two conclusions I make today before I get on the airplane home.
>
> In six months, I'll find some evidence that we had this conversation at all (in my teaching, in some online conversation, in a chance meeting with one of you somewhere else, in a fresh link to this speech on the web).

Are these perfect measures? Of course not. They are horribly flawed and imperfect. But they are useful to me. And if I use them more than once, I can make them slightly more useful each time.

While you're considering those indicators, also consider this: Now that you know what I'm measuring, will you behave differently? Does the attention to an indicator change how we behave together? It's another topic for your inner conference, which we'll get to later.

By now, many of you are likely saying to yourselves: "Get on with it, already! Stop talking about how you're going to talk, and actually talk about something!" Others might have figured out that I've been talking about our conference subject all along the way. Our subject, in a nutshell, is this:

> *If culture counts, how do we count it?*

Or, to say the same thing in far more words:

> If cultural experience and expression offer uniquely powerful value to our lives, our relationships, our communities, and our world, where do we find the residue of that value in a form that's useful to us and compelling to others?

If we follow the process of the beginning of my speech, it doesn't seem all that difficult to do:

1. State what you value out loud;
2. find observable indicators of those values;
3. watch for them to appear or accrete over time; and
4. change your measures as you must.

As cultural professionals, we should be particularly good at this, since we're all in the business of creating meaning, discerning excellence and worth, and conveying both to a wider audience. Better yet, we have thousands of willing helpers to keep us current and keep us honest. We have audiences, volunteers, friends, critics, and supporters.

This should be cake.

But, of course, it's not cake. It's more like soufflé – a process prone to consternation, frustration, and even resentment. Why is this so vexing and so awkward? There are a few obvious answers that we might as well get out of the way:

First, cultural expression is, itself, a "way of knowing." It exists alongside scientific inquiry, the social sciences, and other defined disciplines precisely because it does things that other modes of expression and discovery cannot. As actor/comedian Martin Mull once said: "Writing about music is like dancing about architecture."[44] Any attempt to measure the value of art in some other form (whether scientific measure, social research, economics, and the like) is therefore silly. While this is absolutely true, I'll suggest that we should just move on from this particular point. It's a dead end. It's a conversational sand trap.

The second challenge is that we don't get to pick the essential values or indicators for our community. Our communities have their own values and indicators, thank you very much, and we're left to retrofit them as best we can: educational attainment, for example, or economic development, or social welfare, or civic engagement. These are the values and measures our constituents understand, especially those who decide how to allocate resources and power. While it's nice to dream about defining our own values and indicators, some might say they wouldn't be useful in the world we live in. True? We'll get to this in a minute.

The third barrier to the conversation just struck me last week as I was preparing for our discussion today. Perhaps we are emerging from an era when arts and cultural activity was *itself* an indicator. During the great global competition among socio-political systems, the arts were one of the boasting points lobbed from dignitary to dignitary. Great societies have great art, went the argument. So great art was an *indicator* that your chosen political system was great. Communism and capitalism certainly used that indicator a lot, along with Olympic sport. But I'd suggest that nationalism and boosterism had some significant role to play in the growth of cultural infrastructures around the world, as well – in China, in Europe, and yes, in Canada, too.

In some small corners of the world, this arts-as-indicator mindset is still in active play. In a fabulous news article out of Havana just a week before this talk,[45] Fidel Castro was congratulating a new class of arts educators, and boasting about the arts instructors now present in every one of his island's 4800 schools. Here, in the very first sentence, is an example of the arts as an indicator:

> The conviction that our people have sown the seeds of a better society was shared by President Fidel Castro with the 3,092 arts instructors of the second national graduation in this specialty.

And I can't let that article go by without highlighting Castro's charge to the graduates, which has immediately become the motto of our master's program in Arts Management: "Forward, valiant standard bearers of culture and humanism! A life of glory awaits you!" To be an indicator is a glorious thing. You don't need evidence to prove your value because you are a placeholder for value. You are the goal. You are the absolute good. Just look to Gross National Product as the golden child of modern indicators, or the Nikkei Stock Average in Japan. Whether or not they are the best indicators of social or economic health, they are the measures that are now anointed, and we manage our societies to improve them. Cultural infrastructure, at least in the 1950s, '60s, and '70s, benefited from that indicator status, and perhaps it was in those years that our industry established its persistent sense of self.

But somewhere in the collapse of communism, the national posturing around cultural achievement became less essential (except in Cuba, perhaps). The health and vitality of public and nonprofit arts wasn't an indicator anymore, and slowly arts organizations came to need indicators to prove their public worth by public measures. I suggest that transition began during the 1980s, and continues to ripple around the world today. Whether guised in conversations about privatization of public cultural institutions, allocation of increasingly scarce public funds, or the tension between serving social needs and serving the muse, the discussion challenges our collective sense of self. We shouldn't need indicators, we should *be* indicators!

In the movie *Big Night*, one of my favorite films about cultural management (yes, there are films about cultural management), two Italian-born brothers struggle to keep their family restaurant afloat in 1950s New Jersey. One brother, Primo (Tony Shalhoub), is a consummate artist in the kitchen, a creative genius of cuisine. The other, Secundo (Stanley Tucci), is trapped between the uncompromising artistry of his brother, and the practical reality of running a business: Customers that dare to demand a side of pasta with their risotto and competitors that pander with spaghetti, meatballs, and cheap Chianti. In one wrenching scene for any of us in the arts, Primo says to Secundo: "People should come just for the food." Secundo replies, "I know, but they don't."

It's the same truth for the perceived public value of arts and culture. Public value is not an entitlement. It's a glacial conversation that crosses borders and decades, and we can't sit back and wait for the glacier to ooze again in our direction.

Finally, I'll suggest a fourth barrier to our conversations about measuring value. To my mind, it's the biggest and realest of them all: Indicators are a dangerous game. Indicators, measurements, and metrics can often take on a life of their own. If they're not grounded in or resonant with what we believe to be important, they can pull us and our organizations far off course.

As sustainability advocate and systems guru Donella Meadows wrote:

> We try to measure what we value. We come to value what we measure. The feedback process is common, inevitable, useful, and full of pitfalls.[46]

If we lack a "north star" to keep us on course, what we value and what we measure can blend together, and we can lose our way in the world.

Take, for example, the common metric of growth as a universal indicator of success – more audiences every year, more productions, more exhibits, more endowment, more facilities, more programs, more revenue, more staff. Growth certainly offers us easy indicators to observe over time – headcounts, production days, fund balances, square footage, net revenue, staff rosters. If one or more of these indicators goes up, we must be doing well. If some or all go down, we must be doing poorly.

Of course, that's nuts.

Or, take, for example, the metrics of utility we've come to embrace as an industry over the past decade. Arts for economic impact. Arts for social good. Arts for educational attainment. Arts for personal health. Since contemporary society is riddled with vexing and complex problems, it makes sense to position the arts as problem-solvers. Again, the indicators for these values are measurable – dollars spent and spent again (that glorious multiplier effect), pro-social behavior among at-risk populations, standardized test scores, years of productive life. And they make an effective argument with decision-leaders, especially if we ignore all other activities that might produce similar or even bigger results. Certainly, creative expression and cultural experience have utility to social and personal issues. They do change lives. They do shape communities. They do refocus economic activity…to a point. But utility as an indicator is not the same as utility as a core value.

As Frank Zappa said: "I wrote a song about dental floss but did anyone's teeth get cleaner?"

Audiences don't engage in cultural experience because they seek to refocus economic activity in the urban core. At-risk youth don't stay in theater programs to encourage their pro-social behavior. Students don't play in a school orchestra because they want better spatial reasoning. All these things are byproducts of the true value in what we do. As I said in another speech to another audience, they are the footprints, not the giant (see Chapter 19).

Now, we all want to be useful. Where's the distortion or distraction in wanting our cultural efforts to be useful, as well?

Consider this: What if it is that moment of connection between audience and artist, between artist and art, between a young performer and their performance that is the engine of all utility? What if it is the accumulation of thousands of such moments – moments of awakening, of identity, of discovery, of connection, of meaning – that constitutes the public value of our work?

If that's the case, then turning our attention from that moment to be more useful would actually dissipate our usefulness. And growing to extend our circle just because we think growth is good might leave us hollow at the core.

Indicators are a dangerous game, to be sure. We can lose ourselves and what we value when we measure things around us. But it's not like we have a choice. We are all constantly measuring, whether explicitly or implicitly. It's how we engage our world. Our only choice here is to choose to do so with intention, or without it – in the daylight or in the darkness.

So, how does this all shape the conversation of the next few days? You have the resources and the extraordinary "face time" to shape it any way you like. But as we discuss what value we create with our work, I'd like to suggest some framing statements that might help keep us all honest and on track:

First, value is always a co-construction. It is not something delivered and received, produced and consumed, it is created in the moment it is experienced.

Second, value is always the product of multiple experiences, never just one. That moment of connection may seem like a sudden flash, but it's really the product of an entire lifetime, if not two. The philosopher John Dewey has a wonderful metaphor for this fact in the experience of a lightening flash in an open field.[47] The lightening may have suddenly illuminated our view, he says, but it was our previous life experience that let us recognize the elements of the landscape that were illuminated. Without that previous experience, the flash would have no meaning.

This fact is essential to our measures of value, since no single organization has the power or capacity to generate that value. They can only do so as part of a continuum of experience, and an ecology of opportunity.

Third, we must always remember that future experience has a present value. Preserving the opportunity of cultural experience for those not yet born has an important place in our calculus.

Fourth, all measures are subjective. How we select what to measure, how we measure it, and how we interpret what we find are matters of human perspective and human limits. The physicist Werner Heisenberg had a wonderful way of expressing this fact for his peers in the sciences:

> ...what we observe is not nature itself, but nature exposed to our method of questioning. Our scientific work in physics consists in asking questions about nature in the language we possess.[48]

Of course, we should strive to design around our biases and blind spots – especially by inviting others to participate in the cause. But we should never assume we are being completely objective, and we should hold an honored space for blatantly subjective measures in the mix.

Finally, regardless of our indicators or our metrics, value is where we begin and where we end this conversation. It recalls a stanza from T.S. Eliot's "The Four Quartets" that

I think perfectly describes the journey we're all traveling in this glorious "face time" we have together:

> We shall not cease from exploration
> And the end of all our exploring
> Will be to arrive where we started
> And know the place for the first time.

It's a circular journey I truly look forward to. And I thank you again for your precious time.

Now, let's talk.

This speech was prepared for and presented to the Canadian Association for the Performing Arts/l'Association canadienne des organismes artistiques (CAPACOA) conference, "Culture Counts: Measuring the Value of the Arts," on November 5, 2005, Ottawa, Ontario.

32

THE CONFERENCE PANEL'S PRAYER

Conference panels so often begin in hope and end in entropy. Like many other collective human endeavors, they recur in similar form, again and again, like ritual. But unlike other rituals, they lack an invocation prayer. Here is my offering to summon positive forces and to focus collective attention.

> Our panel,
> which is in progress,
> what the hell is thy point?
> We few convened,
> each question screened,
> both us and them, same as ever.
> Give those on this dais our timely insight.
> And forgive us our fallacies,
> as we forgive those who bring them to our attention.
> Lead us not into polemics,
> but deliver us from tedium.
> For thine is the process of the conference
> in the plenary forever.
> Amen.

Originally posted: June 16, 2014

33

AL PRIEVE AND THE SUM OF THE PARTS

All that I think or write or teach or wonder or learn about the management of cultural organizations connects back to Dr. E. Arthur "Al" Prieve. Not only was he my first professor of Arts Administration, but he was also my on-going reference for how things connect. He passed away in 2014. But his lessons continue.

In 1991, when I first met him, he sketched out the course list for the master's degree I had come to the University of Wisconsin-Madison from Boston to learn about. On a yellow legal pad, with a number two pencil, he wrote the course names for the curriculum he developed – marketing, financial accounting, statistics, organizational behavior, ethics, seminar, and so on. And as he wrote the words, he connected them with a winding narrative, describing how one course influenced the other, and how each element of arts administration comprised a coherent whole.

In 20 minutes, decades ago, he shared a roadmap for cultural management that I'm still exploring today.

I would have some version of the same experience with him over and over during our long years of connection.

Things I saw as pieces, he would frame as connected. People I thought of as individuals, he would describe as family. Even as his memory faltered later in life, he could recall and recount the entire careers of his former students, as well as their life partners, locations, and personal quirks.

Al Prieve was among the first to frame cultural management as an academic pursuit. In the mid-1960s he drew challenge and inspiration from the launch of the National Endowment for the Arts, the growth of foundation funding and community cultural spending across America, and the need for thoughtful and responsive professionals for the rising tide of arts organizations. Course by course, connection by connection, he defined an entire field and the skills required to serve it. And he developed several generations of arts leaders that contribute to its vitality today.

When Al looked at his students, he also saw more than the sum of their parts. He saw potential and passion, and the roles they might contribute to the larger play. And he was always finding elegant ways to weave them into the plot. Somewhere during my graduate studies, he saw some greater sum in me. And he gave me space and encouragement to grow toward it. He hired me as Assistant Director to the Bolz Center for Arts Administration at UW-Madison shortly after I graduated. And he nudged me toward more teaching and writing and thinking and connection with the field, all with his trademark patience, persistence, and grace.

When he retired in 2000, Al championed my appointment as Director. And the network of alumni, practitioners, educators, and insights he had assembled during his decades of generous service made my work a joy. From years of observing him, I knew I could never replace him. But I worked to steward his vision, and to make him proud.

Al Prieve made the world more than the sum of its parts. He was the thread that tied ideas together. He was the keeper and teller of stories that threaded people together. His hand is still now. But his handiwork shimmers on.

Original blog post: March 26, 2014

STRUCTURE & STRATEGY

34

THE THEORY OF STRATEGY

"You keep using that word. I do not think it means what you think it means."

INIGO MONTOYA (via WILLIAM GOLDMAN)

Imagine that there was a commonly held theory of gravity that said objects will fall at an increasing rate, pause halfway, do a little spin, and then continue to fall. Imagine, then, that you never actually observe any object falling in that particular way. A little like that, sure…the falling part. But not exactly like that, and certainly never with that suggested little pause and spin.

Imagine, then, that you asked smart people about this lack of observed evidence, wondering whether the theory might need a revision that matched observations, and they replied: "Well, things *should* fall like that. And if they knew better, they would."

There is a theory much like this, frequently referenced and often espoused, called "strategy." And while there are many special theories of strategy that seem to track with observed evidence, the general theory does not, at all, ever. The general theory says that organizations achieve objectives by defining a clear and measurable goal, considering the range of possible actions toward that goal, implementing the actions that seem most likely to move them forward, and then measuring their progress and adjusting as they go. The General Theory of Strategy is mostly linear, mostly intentional, and mostly about alignment of resources, actions, and desired outcomes.

Problem is, no collective human endeavor ever happens like that. A little like that, sure…the considering and moving and choosing part. But not exactly like that, and certainly never with that suggested clarity and intent. And I don't just mean it never happens in the nonprofit arts. I mean it never happens, anywhere, ever.

Consider the odds against it:

A clear and measurable goal

When have you, as an individual, ever been able to define a perfectly clear and measurable goal? For every action on this earth, you have complex, overlapping, and internally inconsistent goals – some explicit, some implicit, some physical, some emotional, some social. (Should I walk to the water fountain to get a drink? I'm thirsty, yes, but I might run into Bob.) Now, magnify that complexity by the power of two for two people, three for three people, and on and on. We can certainly agree on an explicit, aggregated, or average goal that seems to align with most of our individual and collective goals, but at best it's a fuzzy estimate, and it's dripping with "let's pretend."

Considering the range of possible actions

When have you, in your life, been able to identify, assess, and understand the consequences of all available actions? You can be aware of many possible actions, particularly the ones you've tried before. But you can't possibly know their extended outcomes. And if you could know, you would have the previous problem of overlapping and inconsistent goals making a clear comparison between actions impossible.

As Herbert Simon stated the problem with classical decision theory back in 1979:[49]

> The classical model calls for knowledge of all the alternatives that are open to choice. It calls for complete knowledge of, or ability to compute, the consequences that will follow on each of the alternatives. It calls for certainty in the decision maker's present and future evaluation of these consequences. It calls for the ability to compare consequences, no matter how diverse and heterogeneous, in terms of some consistent measure of utility.

And that's just two elements of the General Theory of Strategy. The rest are worse.

Of course! I hear you say. Nobody *really* thinks strategy is a rigid and real thing. It's an aspiration. A guideline for good behavior that nobody ever actually achieves. A "true north" that guides our way in a murky darkness (strategy conversations always eventually lead to a compass metaphor, usually because strategy inevitably feels like the uncharted wild).

But in the rooms I sit, with funders, board members, academics (yes, I do this myself), consultants, boards, and other boosters of cultural organizations, the General Theory of Strategy is a real and resident thing. Heads are shaken in disdain as we hear and share stories of non-strategy, of messy, confused, staggering, iterative, conflicted processes by arts organizations, so distant from the clear and obvious General Theory of Strategy. These organizations and their occupants don't move the way they *should* move, the way they *would* move if they only knew better.

Often, a business-savvy board member or foundation executive will encourage us to look to the corporate world, where the General Theory of Strategy is both proof and pudding. But even there, we find complex human interactions and imperfections mucking up the beautiful linear. Or, as Henry Mintzberg noticed when he actually observed corporate process:[50]

> ...the choices are made by people who often do not fully comprehend the proposals presented to them. Thus, in authorization the comparative ignorance of the manager is coupled with the inherent bias of the sponsor.

So, no. I'm not suggesting we abandon intent, goal-setting, option-seeking, evaluation, and adjustment in our work. I'm not even suggesting we give up on the word "strategy" as a placeholder for this kind of intentional and pseudo-rational approach. I'm just suggesting that we acknowledge that any and all human processes are sloppy and slippery and riddled with impossible odds, and perhaps be kinder and calmer with others and ourselves about them.

Let's not push and stress so hard on what *should* happen in the pursuit of collective effort. Let's stop and observe, with compassion, what *does* happen, and consider how it might happen better.

Original blog post: February 6, 2015

35
SPOILER ALERT: HUMANS HAVE BODIES

"Our inner experience is as real as stones or electrons and as ordinary an activity for a social mammal as digestion or the circulation of the blood."
MARY MIDGLEY

I began my professional life as an arts management educator in Fall 1995. My focus, since then, has been rather specific: effective management of (mostly) professional (mostly) nonprofit organizations that produce, preserve, present, and support creative human expression. After so many years, it's embarrassing to admit that I've missed a dramatic blind spot in teaching, management, and organizational theory until now:

Humans have bodies.

And yes, I know that I have a body. This isn't news to me. But what has become suddenly obvious is that the founding logics of both the academic and business world assume that we don't have bodies, or that bodies are inconsequential to personal, professional, or civic life.

Sir Ken Robinson remarked on this aspect of academia, and particularly the professors therein:

> There's something curious about professors in my experience – not all of them, but typically, they live in their heads.... They're disembodied, you know, in a kind of literal way. They look upon their body as a form of transport for their heads.... It's a way of getting their head to meetings.[51]

And sure, when you choose to be a university professor, you're selecting a life of the mind...where you spend extra attention and bring focused intention to the intellect. I'm cool with that. Again, this isn't news to me. Professors have long been accused of detachment from reality.

But the news to me is how pervasive this detachment is, not only in academia, but also in business.

On the business side, scholar Antonio Strati observes this bias throughout the history of organizational theory and management studies. And I know I'm talking about theory again, but I've worked with enough businesses and professionals to know that these assumptions are commonly held. Strati makes his point by describing the kind of insane working world these shared theories imply:

> ...as soon as a human person crosses the virtual or physical threshold of an organization, s/he is purged of corporeality, so that only his or her mind remains. Once a person has crossed this threshold, therefore, s/he is stripped of both clothing and body and con-

> sists of pure thought, which the organization equips with work instruments and thus reclothes. When the person leaves the organization, the mind sheds these work instruments and resumes its corporeality, and with it the perceptive faculties and aesthetic judgement that yield aesthetic understanding of reality, but only in the society lying outside the physical or virtual walls of the organization.[52]

Even in academia, that doesn't sound like my institution, nor my job. And thank goodness for that. In my work, I'm informed and deeply affected by my physical environment, by all of my senses and how they make sense with each other, by the muscle memories of my external life, by the sense of myself and my peers occupying space together.

This brain-but-not-body bias is not just bizarre, it can be insidious. Imagine, for example, you decided that a primary goal of public-school education, or university education, was to prepare individuals for the work force, to be productive citizens through employment or entrepreneurship or the like. You would draw on your assumptions about work, organizations, and industry (or ask industry for their assumptions, which would carry this bias too), and design a system that prepares them for that impossible world.

Pure intellect, with participants transported by bodies but unaffected by them, working in systems of pure intellect (sure, complicated by politics and power and such, but all described in rational/cognitive terms).

You'd emphasize the skills of reason – like reading, writing, math – and discount anything sensuous or aesthetic. You might keep the arts, but mostly those elements that appeared to build practical skills, or elements that facilitated learning of the "important" cognitive capacities. But you'd discount anything, including art, that strayed too far into the senses or the physical self. Even further, you might flag those things as contrary to intellect or reason, distractions perhaps, and want them out entirely.

Now, imagine you did this for generations.

As an alternative, let's suppose you believed public school and university education to be intended for something *more* than employment...for whole and purposeful people, with civic vision, global understanding, deep curiosity, and the agency to integrate those things into their lives and societies.

Even then, your deep-seated theories of the world might tilt toward intellect. And you would design an intervention to prepare students for a disconnected and disembodied universe that doesn't actually exist.

Now, imagine you wanted to design and lead an arts organization, a durable collective effort committed to creative human expression, not only of the mind (although sure), but of the whole person or the whole community. As passionate radicals, you might even admit that the artists and audiences you serve have bodies and complex aesthetic selves. But you likely wouldn't extend that admission to yourself or your team, your board, or your business partners. When doing business, you would want to behave "like a business." And people in businesses don't have bodies.

Imagine an organization that disregarded this rather essential bit of human reality. Or perhaps you don't have to imagine it. Perhaps you already work there.

The first step in addressing a bias is acknowledging you have one. I've glimpsed it in myself. I'm admitting I have a problem. I'm stumbling to correct it. And now that I'm looking, I'm sensing it all around me.

Original blog post: January 14, 2016

36

TERRIFYING EFFICIENCY

"All of our social problems arise out of doing the wrong thing righter. The more efficient you are at doing the wrong thing, the wronger you become."
RUSSEL ACKOFF

For as long as I've been observing the arts and culture world through a "systems" lens, I've been frustrated by the number of apparently broken systems. Thoughtful people in experienced communities building cultural facilities that are too large for their goals. Smart individuals making odd and upside-down decisions when part of a governing board. Foundations earnestly leading an entire community or artistic discipline into greater instability with their grants.

Everywhere you look there are systems of people and activities that seem to deliver results contrary to their stated goals. Politics. Education. Philanthropy. City planning. And on and on.

But one day, I started playing a new game when I began to obsess about a broken system. I ignore the stated or assumed goals of the enterprise, and I assume the actual outcomes were exactly the ones intended. In other words, I imagined the system not as broken, but as brutally efficient at delivering some other end.

Take, for example, the construction of extremely large cultural facilities – large in physical size, capital expense, and on-going operational overhead. Often, the stated goals of these capital projects are to increase the vitality and impact of the arts for a community. And yet, equally often, their result is risk-aversion, tighter budgets, higher rents, and a large philanthropic sucking sound drawing resources away from program (variable) expense toward the gaping maw of overhead (fixed) expense.

Mapped against stated goals, massive cultural construction can sound like the result of a broken system. But imagine the alternative view: that the outcome was exactly aligned with intent. Imagine that the chief executive, the lead donors, the project architect, and even the public officials are all inclined toward a bold public space – as large and as technically excellent as current capital will allow. Then the system isn't inefficient, but rather it's terrifyingly efficient at delivering the unstated goal.

As another example, a colleague of mine works hard to energize their community through the arts and artists. A primary challenge has been broken-down storefronts and commercial properties that have fallen below the zoning code, and that desperately require investment and innovation. When we assume that all owners would want a more vital and vibrant use for their property, the system seems oddly resistant to even simple interventions that cost little and could gain much. But what if, instead, the system of broken buildings is actually delivering exactly what's intended (for someone who has a say in the matter)? What if the landlords – often absent or distant owners in search of tax write-offs – prefer a closed and broken neighborhood to an open and active one?

These alternate outcomes don't need to be nefarious or even intentional. But the pull of other intents, or the assumptions about the best means to get there, can certainly play a role in unexpected results.

It's a thinking game, I'll admit. One without consistent utility. But every now and then, it can be extremely useful to consider an apparently broken system as entirely effective, but toward a different end. If your goal is to change the direction of that system toward an alternate outcome or behavior, it's best to know what tidal forces you'll be swimming against.

Original blog post: October 16, 2012

37

MORE PRODUCTIVE, LESS DESTRUCTIVE

"Yet why not say what happened?
Pray for the grace of accuracy
Vermeer gave to the sun's illumination
stealing like the tide across a map
to his girl solid with yearning."

ROBERT LOWELL

One of my favorite moments in any planning or strategy meeting is when someone looks suddenly resolute, and says something like: "You know what the problem is? The problem is that we don't have a system to [do or decide or develop the thing we're talking about]."

I love this moment because, almost always, in the very next sentence they describe in rather sophisticated detail the current system that does that thing. Then everyone in the room nods and agrees that yes, that's how it works now, and no, they don't have a system, and yes, they need one.

There is (almost) always a system that does whatever the thing is. And everyone knows its parts and its processes.

Granted, often that system sucks – it's unproductive and sometimes destructive – but it's there.

I remember discovering this form of public theater decades ago, at a meeting about cultural policy. Many academics, advocates, and funders were around the table, trying to improve access and impact for cultural policy research. And someone became suddenly resolute and said (something like): "You know what the problem is? The problem is that we don't have a system to share and disseminate the most important and relevant research." And then, in the next breath: "Right now, whenever anyone has a question about cultural policy research, they call me or a handful of other researchers, and ask for recommendations or referrals. I'm getting these calls all the time." And the whole room nodded.

We then went on for hours discussing and designing a complex and expensive web-based database of cultural policy research, a system built from scratch to solve the "missing system" problem. And nobody used it. Instead, they kept making calls (and later emails) to a few connected people who could refer them to relevant resources.

Smart, earnest, and well-intentioned people often yearn for fresh-made systems – of information exchange, decision-making, organizational structures, reporting relationships, funding and financing, even cultural production and presentation – when they feel frustrated in their work. Or when they assume that professionals build fresh systems, and figure they should do that too.

But what if, when frustrated or longing to look professional, you explored the existing culture, processes, and practices – often deeply embedded in the enterprise or the community – and asked how to make them work better? What if the goal wasn't a fresh, new, designed-to-specs system, but a more productive and less destructive version of the current way of doing things?

Human systems are more like water than wind-up clocks. They find their way between points not by logic but by paths of least resistance. They bend around obstacles and seep into soft spots. They erode tracks and canyons into those paths by retracing them over time. Sure, those paths can also become entrenchments that need redirection. But why not start with the ways the water flows?

The next time you're in a meeting and someone says, "We don't have a system that...," listen to (and write down) the very next words they say. There's a system in there that might not need reinvention, but rather a bit of attention, cultivation, and care.

Original blog post: April 4, 2017

38
CARROTS AND STICKS

"Starting to think that all the world's major problems can be solved with either oyster sauce or backing vocals."
BRIAN ENO

An often-celebrated and often-debated aspect of Irish tax law provides an income-tax exemption for artists around the sale of their work.[53]

The exemption, designed originally to provide another form of subsidy to creative artists, also became a massive incentive for affluent creative individuals to claim their home (and tax haven) in Ireland.

It's an interesting example of the challenges of carrots and sticks, or the various policies governments use to reshape their cultural landscape (intentionally, or more often by accident). Through income tax incentives, zoning, specialized tax credits (for preservation of historic buildings, for example), grants, awards, marketing, and communications, governments can encourage certain choices over others. In the aggregate, these redirected choices of individuals slowly accumulate into a new shape and face to a community, a city, or a country.

One of the more bizarre elements of Ireland's tax exemption is the burden it places on the government's revenue bureaucracy. Since the legislation provides an exemption to artistic work that is "original and creative" in one of five creative forms (a book or other writing; a play; a musical composition; a painting or other like picture; or a sculpture), it's up to the revenue office to determine what "original and creative" means – a task that would give even an aesthetics professor a conniption.

To resolve this, the legislation defines originality, creativity, truth, and beauty in creative expression, at least for the Irish universe:

> A work shall be regarded as original and creative only if it is a unique work of creative quality brought into existence by the exercise of its creator's imagination.
>
> A work shall be regarded as having cultural merit only if by reason of its quality of form and/or content it enhances to a significant degree one or more aspects of national or international culture.
>
> A work shall be regarded as having artistic merit only if its quality of form and/or content enhances to a significant degree the canon of work in the relevant category.

On the one hand, it's wonderful to know that the definitions of "cultural merit" and "artistic merit" have been resolved by the Irish Office of the Revenue Commissioners. All you humanities and philosophy professors can go home, your work is done.

On the other hand, this legislation raises the question of how, exactly, governments and nonprofits can shape and shift the creative balance of their communities. And there, the toolset is more diverse than you might think:

Distributing cash

The most obvious incentive system involves distributing money. You develop a grant program with certain rules to receive the money (create a new education program, focus more activity in an underserved area, present a certain kind of work), and artists, individuals, and organizations will grow toward the light. Less obvious elements in this toolset include other financial vehicles such as microgrants, loans, monetary awards for good behavior, and such.

Connecting the Dots

Governments, organizations, and individuals can also change their environment by leveraging the efforts of others. They can connect organizations, lobby for such connections, and nudge their friends and associates to move in a certain direction.

Defining Reality

Sometimes, by just defining a hole in your environment with clarity and persuasion, you can help other people see the hole themselves. Aggregating, generating, sharing, and analyzing information about the environment can shape a collective vision of what might be. If you create an obvious and compelling vacuum, it might just suck someone in to fill it.

Convening

A corollary to "connecting the dots" and "defining reality" is the noble art of convening – bringing people together to synchronize their efforts, challenge their progress, or just to broaden their network can have powerful impacts on the shape of a regional culture.

Being an Agent

On the less glamorous side of the spectrum, organizations and governments can assume some of the back-office headaches of individuals or collectives serving the chosen cause. This agency can come in the form of shared infrastructure, shared staff, shared office space, or even shared nonprofit status called fiscal sponsorship. By providing this form of agency and structural support, organizations can encourage more activity by lowering the barriers to joining the fray.

Leveraging the Policy Toolkit

Governments create general incentive systems that can be used to benefit a specific cause (like the arts). If you understand your region's zoning rules, specialized tax credits, development incentives, and the like, you can help arts initiatives reap their benefits. A great example of this is Artspace, which uses low-income housing credits (among other things) to finance artist live/work spaces.[54]

Magnetizing the Environment

If your goal is to attract a certain type of individual or initiative to a community, you can sometimes just create a positive environment that draws them in – through advertisement, branding, public relations, aesthetic improvements, or collective word-of-mouth.

Coercion

There are times when you can force an individual, organization, or group to behave in a certain way. It's not common in the toolbox of nonprofits, but governments can play this card with care. For example, many cities have a requirement that certain public building projects must allocate a portion of their construction expense to public art. Even outside of government, organizations that license or certify can make requirements, as well.

Do It Yourself

Even more obvious than all of the above is to fill the hole yourself. Municipal governments are often the local landlord of arts facilities (especially outside urban areas). They can also be the presenter and em-

> ployer of creative workers. While this path can be the most expensive and challenging, it's often the only way through.

There's one major warning that should be emblazoned on the toolbox, however: beware of success. In a complex world, you can never change just one thing. As you monkey with the ecosystem around you, always be aware of what *other* outcomes your work might spin out. If you're not careful, you might destroy or distort the cause you had hoped to support.

Original blog post: January 4, 2005

39

A HAMMER OR A SPONGE?

"Tools are for people who have nothing better to do than think things through and make sensible plans."
LAINI TAYLOR

I take part in many fascinating conversations about "new business models for the arts." The general set-up is usually that the nonprofit corporate form is showing some wear, and that the downsides of the model (its tendency toward under-capitalization, organizational isolation, plodding governance structures, cumbersome and demanding funding sources, etc.) are coming to outweigh the benefits.

Our impulse for framing the question is to ask what other business models are available. If the 501(c)3 is not the future of the arts, then what? But, as is often the case, that impulse question may be leading us in unproductive directions.

Imagine that you're working at a hardware store, and a customer comes in with a basic question: "Should I use a hammer or a sponge?"

Odds are, since you're a good hardware store clerk, the first response out of your mouth would be another question: "What, exactly, do you need to do?" A hammer is quite useful for certain tasks, and quite useless for soaking up water. A sponge is also effective when set to an appropriate use, but not great at pounding in a nail. For some jobs, it would be wise to have both tools, and some other tools, as well.

The question about the next business model for the non-market-supported arts is quite similar to the hardware customer's question. What business model should you use? What, exactly, do you want to do?

There are dozens of corporate and organizational forms, and thousands of combinations of those forms: S Corporation, C Corporation, LLC, LLP, sole proprietorship, non-stock corporation, unincorporated group, impromptu gathering, municipal entity, quasi-governmental authority, subsidiary, fiscal sponsor, etc. None of these are particularly new. And all of them can be useful tools for advancing a creative cause. Further, the traditional nonprofit form still is quite handy, as well, and will often play a part in the final mix.

As is common in human endeavor (but particularly common to the nonprofit arts) we seem to have confused the tools we use with the job we had in mind. We are not about the nonprofit structure, we are about the artist, the audience, the art, and the places where they meet. We just use that corporate form to accomplish our goals.

So perhaps when we find ourselves considering the *next* business model for the arts, we should pause our mad dash toward business models and, instead, describe what we want to accomplish, and the barriers and opportunities that stand in our way. There are plenty of tools available to us, and through policy we can even make more. But first, we need to describe the task.

Original blog post: April 12, 2005

40

BUILDING STALE METAPHORS IN STONE

"They follow in the beaten track,
And out and in, and forth and back,
And still their devious course pursue,
To keep the path that others do."
SAM WALTER FOSS

The design and construction of a new cultural facility is a unique moment in the life of an arts organization or arts community. It's a chance to rethink how arts and audiences connect, how works are produced, how thriving ecologies of innovation and meaningful experience are structured and sustained.

But there's a fascinating tension in cultural facility design between what might be possible with a clean slate, and what our artistic and management traditions tell us will work.

Case in point: the design of the modern box office. I've seen more than one brand new performing arts space with a box office that looks like an age-old box office – fully enclosed, teller windows, separation glass, stanchions, and velvet rope to mark the place to stand in line. They are built in beautiful stone and glass, I'll admit, but they are nonetheless ossified evidence of an old metaphor: box office as bank.

In the olden days, box offices were centers of cash transactions, requiring high security, complete isolation between tellers, and immovable blast walls between patron and staff. Even though the cash transaction is all but gone for ticket purchases, the metaphor remains: we are secure, we are separate, we are transactional, we don't trust you...get in line.

Yet if you enter an upscale bank these days, you'll see a different metaphor at work: sofas, sitting areas, carpeting, countertops rather than teller windows. In some cases, there aren't tellers at all, just personal financial assistants at desks or tables. The symbolism isn't intimidation, but personal attention and service. For an example, read this description of a bank in Portland, offered by its design firm:

> Part upscale hotel, part retail (and a little bank), Umpqua's innovative new store invites customers to read the paper, enjoy a free cup of coffee, surf the Internet, and shop for banking products. While some banks discourage customers from entering a bank branch and other banks compete against the Internet to provide convenience and speed, Umpqua's new store inspires and encourages its customers to relax and take their time when making financial decisions.

So, why can't a cultural facility team rethink its ticket office in a similar way? The design consultants will likely point at the current box office staff, saying "we tried to show them a new way to conceive of their sales area, but they are luddites." The current box office staff will likely point at the expensive design consultants, saying, "they offered systems that would break, that weren't tested, and that cost an arm and a leg to build and operate...we're running a revenue center here. And we know what works."

Of course, they are both right. The box office must often be a machine of efficiency, and has important elements of transaction. But, as more patrons buy tickets on-line, and as fewer (if any) use cash, the rigid security and separateness of a ticket sales area isn't necessary anymore.

Consider, for example, the Museum of Modern Art in New York, where the admissions area is just a large social space with several long tables. During business hours, these are the membership and ticketing stations. After hours, all equipment is tucked away to make reception space, and the transaction tables become buffets and bars.

Or, even more radical, why have a box office at all? The same functions could be managed by a web site, a phone center, and a roving band of service representatives carrying handheld devices.

That may not be the answer. But it's clear we need better questions before encoding our conventions and metaphors into stone.

Original blog post: April 20, 2005

41

THE ADJACENT POSSIBLE

"The adjacent possible is a kind of shadow future, hovering on the edges of the present state of things, a map of all the ways in which the present can reinvent itself..."

STEVEN JOHNSON

So much of leadership, management, and change narrative is about "gap analysis." The thinking goes that we achieve a desired future by describing a bold vision, defining our current location, mapping the gap between here and there, and then planning and adjusting our route at checkpoints along the way.

This is what grant proposals and change strategies assume and describe. This is what mission, vision, and value statements are designed to serve. But this is also orienteering, which works only when you have a working compass, an adequate map, and a reasonable expectation of persistent terrain.

But what if you and your colleagues are not independent travelers on a static landscape? What if the travelers, the terrain, the compass, and the map all change each other in ways you can't unbundle? And what if describing an optimal and aspirational future tells you nothing about how to take a next step, and might even blind you to other futures?

In that decision space, all you have is the current reality and the available options immediately around you. Theoretical biologist Stuart Kauffman calls this space the "adjacent possible," and considers it an essential part and partner of natural selection. Says he:

> It just may be the case that biospheres on average keep expanding into the adjacent possible. By doing so they increase the diversity of what can happen next.[55]

Evolution doesn't have a "true north" or a long-range target. Rather, the natural world has an array of options it explores with whatever traits or tricks it can bring to bear. Steven Johnson adapts Kauffman's idea to innovation and creativity in his book *Where Good Ideas Come From*, where he writes:

> The history of cultural progress is, almost without exception, a story of one door leading to another door, exploring the palace one room at a time.[56]

So how does this all provide an alternative to "gap analysis" in management and leadership? Management consultant Dave Snowden suggests that rather than describing an idealized distant future and mapping the way (which he finds to be ludicrous in a complex system), we instead should attend to current, everyday stories, and listen for their qualities and impacts. Some stories will show positive motion toward a more productive reality. Others will show negative motion toward a less productive or more destructive reality. The manager's job is then to ask, "what can I do tomorrow to create more of the positive story and less of the negative one?" And door-by-door you move through (and construct) the palace. Says Snowden:

> We need to start doing small things in the present rather than promising massive things in the future.[57]

This approach is less about managing to long-term outcomes, and more about moving through immediate-term vectors. In environments without a working compass, an adequate map, or a persistent terrain (which is pretty much every environment these days), exploring the adjacent possible might be the only kind of movement that gets you somewhere new.

Original blog post: February 27, 2018

42
THE BOX

"The brain is wider than the sky,
For, put them side by side,
The one the other will contain
With ease, and you beside."
EMILY DICKINSON

Sometimes when we try to talk our way out of a problem, we end up reinforcing the problem...or even making it worse. Such is the case with "the box," that clever phrase that rose to prominence at arts conferences and conventions in the '80s and '90s, and that lives on today. Thinking "outside of the box," or "beyond the box," became a professional pastime of arts managers and keynoters over the past decades, usually making its comeback during tough economic times.

The frustrating reality of negating something, however, is that you actually strengthen its hold. If I suggest that you *not* think of a giraffe right now, what pops into your head?

Okay, now don't think of the walls around you that block your creative thinking, ignore the barbed wire between you and an integrated response to your current challenges, and whatever you do, don't feel a sense of helplessness and loss of energy in your professional life.

There, didn't that help?

With all the focus on "the box," we often forget that there is no box. It's a fiction. It's a metaphor. It's a catchy phrase for a conference brochure. There certainly can be limits that keep us from seeing a wider world of possibilities – limits like social and psychological blind spots, inflexible assumptions, groupthink, and entrenched "common knowledge." But these limits are much more malleable, variable, and actionable than "the box" implies.

Perhaps the first step in thinking outside the box is to stop talking about the box. It's a construct that we constructed ourselves, and we only make it stronger by plotting our escape.

Original blog post: August 11, 2003

43
CURIOUSER AND CURIOUSER

"Curiosity, like coffee, is an acquired need. Just a titillation at the beginning, it becomes with training a raging passion."
NICHOLAS S. THOMPSON

In 2014, I had the pleasure of keynoting the CAPACOA conference in Toronto – a charming bundle of Canadian performing arts presenters, managers, artists, and related professionals. The topic, as assigned, was *curiosity,* which led me to wonder a few things: what is curiosity, how does it work, and what might cultural managers do differently if they knew some answers to question one and two?

The Oxford English Dictionary offers two subjective uses of the word "curiosity" (ignoring for now the objective uses). One positive: "The desire or inclination to know or learn about anything, esp. what is novel or strange; a feeling of interest leading one to inquire about anything." One decidedly sinister: "The disposition to inquire too minutely into anything; undue or inquisitive desire to know or learn."

So, curiosity can drive us to learn more about our world and its inhabitants, sometimes more intensely than the moment requires. We all want our audiences and communities to be more curious, particularly about our work and the things we care about. But we don't want the fickle and salacious curiosity that would draw them quickly elsewhere.

For the conversation in Toronto, I adopted and adapted a definition from behavioral psychology (specifically from Carnegie Mellon's George Loewenstein):

> Curiosity is the hunger that arises when attention becomes focused on a gap in what you know.[58]

The frame offers several useful insights:

> *That curiosity is deeply related to what you know.* Several studies suggest that more you know about a domain, the more curious you are about the elements you don't know.

> *That attention is also an essential part of the puzzle.* We all have lots of gaps in our knowledge, but we become curious when our attention is focused on a particular gap.

> *That hunger is one of many possible responses to our attention to the gap*, others being aversion, fear, or apathy.

> *That our perception of the gap is essential to that emotional response* – how big we think it is, what capacity we identify in ourselves or our environment to bridge it, and what pleasure we expect if we get to the other side.

For the CAPACOA convening, I offered six strategies to nurture curiosity within ourselves, our co-workers, and our communities:

> *The Question*
> The easiest way to pull focus toward a gap in what we know is to ask a question. If we consider the other aspects of curiosity above, we'd be thoughtful to ask a well-framed question that invites rather than intimidates, and that encourages people to believe the answer is within reach.
>
> *The Sequence or Story*
> Our brains are pattern-seeking machines, which makes an unfolding sequence of events particularly compelling. Obviously, art in many forms is driven by story, so our job becomes finding the best way in.
>
> *The Surprise or Disconfirmation*
> Violated expectations turn out to be a powerful way to draw attention and trigger curiosity…when our pattern-guessing brains discover they're mistaken. This is a foundational aspect of comedy – the sudden

and unexpected shift in frame or focus. This is also central to aesthetic experience, in the ways artistic experiences engage and confound our expectations. In our organizations, the habit of seeking disconfirming information can keep us from becoming static and tradition bound.

The Others

Research suggests that we can be motivated toward curiosity when we know that other people know something we don't know. Of course, you want to be kind and careful when invoking this lure. But it's a powerful one.

The Unfinished…

As pattern-seekers, we are also often pattern *makers*…striving to see the whole when shown only the parts. Leaving our work and our messages slightly unfinished can compel people to complete the picture themselves.

The Informed or Reframed Domain

Since we're more likely to be curious within a domain we know, entirely new or foreign domains can leave us cold or cautious about leaning in. If we're seeking to engage people who do not know our work, we can either help them know it, or we can reframe the work in a way that they recognize. Instead of framing our domain as contemporary dance, or theater, or visual

> art, or world music, we can talk about everyday beauty, loss, joy, movement through space, discipline, tradition, or the like.[59]

In short, all of these techniques or tactics to nurture curiosity require us to *be* curious in genuine and even compulsive ways. We need to know, and *want* to know, what frames the lives around us, the people we work with, the communities we seek to serve.

So, if you care about curiosity, begin with a question. And then find the gap that draws you forward.

Original blog post: January 31, 2014

44

DA VINCI'S BFF, THE CPA

"The noblest pleasure is the joy of understanding."
LEONARDO DA VINCI

It's common modern practice to consider art and commerce in tension with each other, with artists and accountants as cartoonish polar opposites. But it wasn't always so. About five centuries ago, art and commerce, artist and accountant, lived with and learned from each other through the lives of Luca Pacioli and an up-and-comer named Leonardo da Vinci.

Da Vinci was, of course, the evolving archetype of the "universal genius," blazing trails as an inventor, painter, sculptor, musician, anatomist, astronomer, and on and on. Pacioli was a scholar, teacher, and bestselling author in mathematics and geometry who had, among other things, clarified and codified double-entry bookkeeping.

Da Vinci had taught himself mathematics and linear perspective from Pacioli's *Summa de arithmetica, geometria, proportioni et proportionalita*, first printed in 1494. Two years later, da Vinci convinced his patron to invite Pacioli to Milan as part of an early "creative placemaking" initiative. While there, the two learned from and supported each other: Pacioli advised da Vinci on perspective and proportion for his large commission of the time, "The Last Supper"; da Vinci provided illustrations for Pacioli's second book, the *De devina proportione*, an early treatise on perspective in painting. Following the French invasion of Milan in 1499, the two escaped to Mantua, where they shared a house for several years.

Da Vinci's impact on art, science, and culture are well known. But Pacioli's contributions were comparably transformative. He combined experience in commercial and university mathematics with scholarship in Greek and medieval Latin math as well as Hindu and Arabic innovations, such as arithmetic, algebra, and the ten digits 0 through 9. He published early insights on perspective, including the "Golden Ratio," that da Vinci and others used to transform visual art and architecture.

But Pacioli is most famous (certainly among CPAs) for a 27-page section of his *Summa*, where he explained, systematized, and extended the bookkeeping practices of Venice, popularizing the double-entry accounting system that still defines modern commerce. The larger book was among the first blockbusters of the publishing world, among the first to get an author's copyright (and an extension for the second printing), and among the first to be written in vernacular rather than Latin (Pacioli wrote: "I have written it so that it may bring advantage and pleasure to those who in literature are learned or not").

In a wider frame, both da Vinci and Pacioli transformed how we humans consider and conceive our individual relationships with the wider world. Through perspective in painting and architecture, da Vinci put the individual in direct relation to nature and the built environment, initiating "point of view" as a core principle of human thought and experience. Through double-entry accounting, Pacioli put individuals and institutions in direct relation to the dynamic systems of their businesses, initiating profit and loss, the income statement, and the balance sheet as means to measure and monitor a firm's success.

In short, da Vinci helped bring us a new perspective on self, while Pacioli helped bring us a new perspective on wealth. We've been building on (and untangling) the implications ever since.[60]

Original blog post: February 21, 2018

45
ALL REVENUE COMES AT A COST

"You think because you understand 'one' you must also understand 'two,' because one and one make two. But you must also understand 'and'."

MAWLANA JALAL-AL-DIN RUMI

It is a natural state of being in a nonprofit arts organization to be searching for more and different sources of revenue. Nonprofits are nonprofits, after all, because they produce or present or preserve work that costs more than it can generate in direct revenue. So there's always a gap between direct revenue and expenses. And that gap yawps constantly, like a hungry pup. Yawp.

But so often when I hear arts groups (boards, staff, artists, whatever) talk about potential revenue sources, they skip a rather essential truth: all revenue comes at a cost. Whether it's earned or contributed, through direct activity or side venture, as a gift or a grant or a subsidy, every nickel of revenue costs you something to discover and receive. Those costs can come in many forms:

Time and attention: While you're chasing revenue, you could have been chasing something else. Sometimes that "something else" is the mission and purposes of your organization.

Overhead and infrastructure: Every action requires an actor, and over time the search for revenue can change the balance of an organization from artistic to administrative actors. This isn't necessarily a bad change, just one that alters the cost and shape of doing business.

Nature of relationships: Financial exchange often defines and refines the relationship between individuals – sometimes harmlessly and in complete alignment with existing relationships, sometimes not. It's essential to understand how new streams of revenue will alter the existing relationships required for healthy operations.

Promises and purposes: Sometimes new revenue comes with strings attached – with contractual requirements on how, when, and where you can spend it. If those requirements align with your work, your timeline, and your cash flow, hurray for you! If not, you've added cost and complexity to your life.

Actual cost: New streams of revenue generally require new processes, policies, systems, and people, all of which can add financial cost – both fixed and variable.

The key, of course, is finding and developing revenue streams that exceed their total cost. And because you're in a nonprofit, such streams are necessarily difficult to find.

As a first step, it helps to be constantly alert to the obvious and hidden costs of any action, and to bring that awareness into your conversations with artists, staff, board, and constituents. Does that new dollar cost you more than a dollar to receive? And if so, does it at least move you forward on your mission, rather than sending you sideways?

Original blog post: July 22, 2013

46

ARTS ENTREPRENEURSHIP VS. THE SUM OF ITS PARTS

"The system is not the sum of the behavior of its parts. It is the product of their interaction."

RUSSELL ACKOFF

Arts entrepreneurship, like its close relative *arts management*, has a complex pedigree and a sprawling footprint. Its frameworks and practices span many disciplines. Its areas of focus include the person, the process, and the outcome of entrepreneurial effort. But while we argue about the various branches and twists of this evolving ecosystem, we may be missing the forest for the trees.

As an older sibling of arts entrepreneurship, arts management offers some useful markers to find our way. Arts management has been aptly labeled a "borrower's field"[61] as it draws from many disciplines in both theory and practice – visual and performing arts, humanities, business, political science, social science, and on and on. But arts management could also be labeled a "burrower's field" as its practitioners, scholars, and supporters often dig their way into emerging and established domains in search of money, shelter, and positive attention.

Centuries ago, the arts found support by burrowing toward the values and vanities of affluent merchants, nobility, or organized religion, and borrowing the trappings of status and class. In the mid-20th Century, artists and arts organizations burrowed toward public purpose, growing philanthropic wealth, and nationalism, borrowing the tools and tactics of the evolving not-for-profit sector. More recently, the arts have burrowed into urban renewal, educational achievement, health and wellness, social cohesion, and a range of other favored foci of philanthropy and policy, often borrowing the processes and practices of each related field.

So it's no wonder that "arts entrepreneurship" faces a similar kerfuffle about what it is and what it isn't, and how we might practice, promote, or study it. The larger concept of entrepreneurship is certainly burrow-worthy as the current coin of the realm for many donors, investors, funding crowds, policy makers, and college administrators seeking same. Entrepreneurship has also proven borrow-worthy, with an evolving set of processes and practices holding deep resonance with creative endeavor, and particular value to passion-rich but resource-poor initiatives.

But what are we talking about when we're talking about entrepreneurship? And what are the unique and specific attributes of arts entrepreneurship? In his Delphi study on the first question, William Gartner identified eight themes that ran through various definitions of entrepreneurship.[62] The themes (as I sort them) focused on the *person* (The Entrepreneur, The Owner-Manager), the *process* (Innovation, Organization Creation, Uniqueness), or the *outcome* (Creating Value, Growth, and Innovation serving as both process and outcome).[63] These three perspectives on entrepreneurship track well with evolving discourse, which explores the qualities and attributes of entrepreneurial individuals and groups (person), the iterative and innovative methods of acquiring and integrating resources (process), and the unique and emergent forms of value created (outcome).

However, understanding the reasons for and reach of arts entrepreneurship's sprawling identity only helps us see the trees. The forest is defined by how its elements are inseparably intertwined.

What if the unique and compelling aspect of arts entrepreneurship is not its separate parts, nor the paths between them, but its complete integration as a system? What if the person, the process, and the outcome inform and transform each other in ways we cannot observe or explain when considering them separately?

Systems scholar Russell Ackoff insisted that a "system is more than the sum of its parts; it is an indivisible whole. It loses its essential properties when it is taken apart."[64] Christian Bruyat and Pierre-André Julien suggest a similar perspective when they emphasize entrepreneurship as an inseparable dialogue between the individual and the new venture creation, where both are transformed and transforming. To them, "entrepreneurship is concerned first and foremost with a process of change, emergence, and creation: creation of new value, but also, and at the same time, change and creation for the individual."[65]

There is potential in the perspective that arts entrepreneurship cannot be defined by the traveler, the road, the destination, or the map, but rather by the journey that combines them all.

This article was originally published in Artivate: A Journal of Entrepreneurship in the Arts *4, no. 1 (Winter 2015): 3–4.*

47

THE COMPONENTS OF RISK

"Risk: A state of uncertainty where some of the possibilities involve a loss, catastrophe, or other undesirable outcome."

DOUGLAS W. HUBBARD

A lot of arts discussions wander around the question of risk. Most are about risk-taking in audiences or communities. Some are about risk tolerance and philanthropy. In these conversations, our language suggests that risk is a single variable, and that the individual is the best unit of analysis (a person is generically either risk-averse, risk-tolerant, or risk-seeking). But that proves to be an inelegant and unproductive path.

Rather than being a personal trait that is somehow encoded within us, "risk" is more like the intersection of multiple factors within and around us. Specifically, risk relates to our *confidence* about an outcome to a situation or experience (aka, our predictive ability or uncertainty). It also relates to our perceived *capacity* to bridge the uncertainty (which informs our confidence, but also has unique dynamics). And it involves our expectation of *consequence* – either for successfully bridging the distance, or for falling short. These aspects aren't exclusively internal or external but are instead conversations between our internal and external worlds. So, our assessment and reaction to "risk" can change as we change, and as our situation changes.

You could think of *confidence* as the distance to be leaped (the farther the jump, the less we can predict what's on the other side), of *capacity* as our perceived or experienced ability to jump and the resources available to help us jump successfully, and of *consequence* as the depth of the chasm between us and the other side (measured against the pleasure awaiting us if we make it).

The word "risk" comes from the French word for "danger." But even danger is a context- and person-specific noun. Lighting a match on an open beach isn't as dangerous as lighting it in a hay-barn near a leaking propane tank. And your capacity to light a match without dropping it or burning your fingers also informs the danger or risk. Finally, your confidence about predicting the outcome of dragging the match across a rough surface in that environment rounds the circle.

So, if you're seeking to inform risk tolerance or risk response – of audiences, artists, funders, board members, administrators, civic leaders, and such – you've got multiple variables to manage and probably multiple problems to solve. Let's explore the variables in a bit more detail:

Confidence

Here I mean certainty about predicted outcomes, not the "can-do" quality of self-help books or *Sound of Music* songs. Our brains, as it turns out, are rather sophisticated "prediction machines," constantly guessing about the next moment, or the trajectory of various variables in space and time. Most of this we do subconsciously, so we're not aware of how much we're doing. Our ability to correctly predict outcomes depends quite a bit on our experience in certain situations or domains. A professional baseball player can make a good guess of the speed and location of a pitch as it's leaving the pitcher's hand. A novice will have no clue. Predictive ability also connects to our innate or developed abilities, or even our multiple intelligences. That same professional baseball player may be a complete wreck when navigating a complex social situation or cocktail reception.

Capacity

Our perceived or experienced capacity to engage an unknown or a potential danger also has multiple parts. It involves our assessment of our own ability, but also our assessment of the environment. (Is there someone to help me? Will I be caught on the other side? Do I see tools available to increase my chance of success? Have other people like me made it?)

Consequence

This variable is a combination of the upside of success (pleasure, reward, return) and the downside of failure (death, disappointment, social ridicule, fi-

> nancial loss). If you are considering a long jump to a nice reward (ice cream on the other side), it matters whether there's a small indent between the lines, or a 100-foot-deep crevasse. If you don't like ice cream (what's wrong with you?), there's no need to make the jump at all. Clay Shirky offers a great perspective on two approaches to avoiding bad consequences: we can work to reduce the *possibility of failure* (by vetting and filtering early on) or the *cost of failure* (by making safe-to-fail experiments or building slack into our systems).[66]

If these variables are useful, then an arts organization has many paths toward fostering different risk responses in audiences, artists, administrators, and others. We can influence the *confidence* or predictive abilities through experience, exposition, and expression. We can influence *capacity* by offering tools, resources, and human support for those eager to explore the unknown. We can influence *consequence* by defining and delivering the upside more effectively and mediating the downside.

Finally, we can open our approach to recognize that people, by themselves, are not risk averse or risk seeking (although they may have tendencies or propensities). Rather, risk is a product of people in context in time.

Original blog post: February 19, 2014

48

BUILD, BUY, OR BOLSTER

"Every time you spend money, you're casting a vote for the kind of world you want."
ANNA LAPPÉ

There are a slew of confusions for nonprofits, and their supporters, that blur the difference between operating money and capital. Even though we may know instinctively that long-term investments and daily operational expenses are different things, we flow them together in our accounting statements, in our planning, in our strategy, and in our brains. Unfortunately, the outcome isn't just about semantics. It's about solvency.

One of the more elegant, therefore most useful, discussions of the issue comes from the Nonprofit Finance Fund, and the distinction between "building" and "buying" in the nonprofit world.[67]

In short, in the world of contributed income, "buying" is about a donor purchasing goods or services as they're already being produced by the enterprise – often on behalf of someone else (tickets to an educational performance for school children, for example). "Building" is about a donor funding changes to the enterprise – to finance its startup and early operations, to restructure the business, to launch a new initiative, to scale into a new region or line of work.

"Buying" is familiar to almost any funder: "We like what you're doing, and we'd like to make it available to more people." Or, "we like what you're doing and know you can't cover your full costs from those you serve, so we'll pay the difference." "Building" can often *look* like buying, but carries with it significant effort to change: "We'd like you to serve a different audience in a different place in a different way." Or, "we'd like you to do your work in a bigger, better facility." Building also requires a longer-term commitment from the funder, or a group of funders, because it essentially destabilizes an organization on purpose, to coax it toward a different relationship with the world.

As one example in the arts, The National Capitalization Project from Grantmakers in the Arts was, in part, training funders to know the difference between building and buying, while also being smart about funding healthy organizations as well as interesting projects.[68]

But in all my reading and conversation about capitalization in the nonprofit arts, it feels as if there's a category missing from building or buying, and that's "bolstering." Bolstering is essentially buying with the added intent of organizational health. It's not seeking change, but rather supporting a healthier version of the current enterprise at its current scale. It's packing a little extra liquidity on the balance sheet, covering *full* cost of the good or service, rather than incremental costs. It's making the delivery of the existing goods or services a bit more sane, humane, and reliable.

So often, a funder will buy a service from a nonprofit on behalf of another party, but not cover the full costs. They'll pay the face value of the ticket, for example, when that value is already discounted by subsidy or market concerns. It's like the early days of Amazon, when every sale meant a loss, so more sales made the loss larger. Or, it's like that classic Saturday Night Live commercial parody of the bank that only made change ("All the time our customers ask us, how do you make money doing this? The answer is simple: volume.").

And it's not just important for the funder to know the difference between buying, building, and bolstering, it's important for the organization too. If we pour all these different types of money into the same bucket, we'll continually be confused about the true dynamics of how we do our work.

Original blog post: November 13, 2013

49

CARRYING COSTS

"...perfection is finally attained not when there is no longer anything to add, but when there is no longer anything to take away."

ANTOINE DE SAINT-EXUPÉRY

In the for-profit world, there's a category of expense called "carrying costs," which includes all costs involved in holding an asset (inventory, for example, which costs money even when it's sitting in the stock room...insurance, security, spoilage, storage, finance, and such). The game in inventory-based businesses is to balance your carrying costs against the cost of not having that thing available when you need it.

If you hold inventory that never turns, you'll eat your profits with carrying costs. But if you suddenly have a bump in sales and run out of inventory, you'll lose all the profit you would have made.

As it turns out, there are a few good reasons for holding more stock than you can immediately sell, and for eating the carrying costs in the process. Among these reasons are the following types of stock:

Cycle Stock: Inventory you hold because you'll need it to service expected sales, based on past experience.

Safety Stock: Inventory you hold in case of unexpected delays or problems in your supply chain...also called "buffer stock."

Speculation Stock: Inventory held in expectation of seasonal or increasing demand. If you're betting that sales will increase, you can buy a bunch of extra stock, perhaps at a bulk discount.

Psychic Stock (my personal favorite): Inventory carried to stimulate demand through display. Customers can't purchase what they don't see (or usually don't), and more stock increases the odds they'll see it. Next time you're in a grocery store, observe the shock-and-awe wall of Campbell's soup. That's psychic stock.

So, why am I sharing this lesson in inventory strategy? Because "carrying cost" is also a rather useful concept for any assets or capacity in an arts organization. As nonprofits, we are inclined to minimize our capacity to the absolute bone...few staff doing lots of work, buildings falling into disrepair, budgets that balance to zero every year instead of building a working reserve. Or, on the flip side, we build or buy assets without considering their carrying costs (massive new cultural facility, anyone?), and then wonder why we're dragging so much weight.

As in the inventory business, carrying too few assets (staff, facilities, technology, savings) leaves us less able to absorb an unexpected shock, or to benefit from an unexpected opportunity. Carrying too many assets bleeds our energy through carrying costs, which also leaves us vulnerable, or slow, or distracted.

Also, as in the inventory business, there's no single correct balance...it's a matter of continual and intentional effort. It's also a matter of designing our organizations so they can ramp up quickly and wind down quickly as external forces demand – through partnerships, good relationships with our suppliers, and nimble staff structures. And finally, what helps in all of this is better information, clearer thinking, and ever more brilliant guessing.

Suddenly, I want soup.

Original blog post: January 30, 2013

50
ORGANIZATIONS DON'T EVOLVE, THEY COPE

"All we control is how we react, and how we recover."
JASON ROBERT BROWN

Due to my profession and my preferences, I end up in a lot of conversations about the "next evolution" of arts organizations. The board-governed, professionally managed, mixed-diet (earned and contributed), high-fixed-cost nonprofit organization seems increasingly ill-equipped for its changing environment. It seems a creature of a previous ecosystem. It seems in need of evolution. Yet, therein lies the problem.

These conversations tend to circle around metaphors from the natural world (as demonstrated above), focusing on ecosystems, environmental changes, and delayed evolution. But I'm coming to realize that we're playing a bit fast and loose with the metaphors. We're calling on existing organizations to evolve to the new environment, as living organisms evolve to theirs. Only, individual organisms don't evolve. They only cope.

Individual organisms are stuck with whatever bundle of traits, abilities, internal systems, and sensory structures they were dealt at birth. They don't evolve during their lifetime. Their species evolves over generations as the natural systems around them select whichever mutation (or lack of mutation) lives to reproduce. Evolution isn't individual and responsive, it's multi-generational and selective.

So, we can tell a nonprofit corporate organization to evolve just as effectively as we can tell a fish to grow opposable thumbs. Its traits and tendencies were inherited at birth. It can adjust its tendencies, it can retrain its reflexes, but it's still a nonprofit corporate organization, even if it can do new tricks.

Of course, a nonprofit and a fish are slightly different. I'll grant you that. An organization is a bundle of people, things, processes, and traditions, bound by contracts and covenants, and restricted in its operation by laws, codes, and norms. A fish is, well, a fish. But while the people, things, and processes can be rearranged, the underlying structures and relationships that determine fundamental behavior remain the same.

It might help to remember that the professional cultural nonprofit organization was, itself, an evolutionary species once, selected to thrive and reproduce by civic and social institutions (the mutation was ideal for an increasingly rich, primordial funding ooze of foundations, governments, and individual wealth in the 1960s, '70s, '80s, and '90s).

But now, that primordial ooze has dried up or attached itself to other species in other pools. And professional nonprofit arts organizations are stuck with the same deck they were dealt when they were founded.

I'm not suggesting we should abandon professional nonprofits and generate mutations in their stead (although, a few mutations might be worth a shot). I'm just suggesting we should stop screaming at individual organizations to evolve. They can't.

Existing organizations can cope. They can adjust on the margins. They can eat a bit less and produce a bit more if they move more elegantly. And many can thrive with their old systems in the new world if they're nimble and resourceful and environmentally lucky. As there's a next generation, we can take care that they're constructed for the new reality, rather than aligned with the old.

And somewhere in there, the system will evolve, as systems do, toward the benefit or detriment of the critters already in the pond.

Original blog post: April 11, 2013

AFTERWORDS

ENDNOTES

1 Hurston, Zora Neale. *Dust Tracks on a Road*. New York: Virago, 2019.

2 I stole/adapted that last line of the blog's purpose statement from Canadian media mogul Moses Znaimer, who said often that "… television is not a problem to be managed, but an instrument to be played." One such citation: Cowan, Jennifer. "The Sheer Force of Attitude." *Wired*, June 1, 1993. https://www.wired.com/1993/06/citytv/.

3 Collins, Jim. *Good to Great and the Social Sectors: Why Business Thinking Is Not the Answer*. Illustrated Edition. Boulder: HarperCollins, 2005.

4 Smith, Mark, and Linda Wheeldon. "High Level Processing Scope in Spoken Sentence Production." *Cognition* 73, no. 3 (December 17, 1999): 205–46.

5 Forster, E. M. *Two Cheers for Democracy*. [1st American ed.]. Harvest Book ; .HB46. New York: Harcourt, Brace, 1951.

6 A notable exception is WolfBrown's work on "intrinsic impacts," which defines and develops many qualities similar to Beardsley's and applies them to audience research.

7 Beardsley, Monroe Curtis. *The Aesthetic Point of View: Selected Essays*. Ithaca, N.Y: Cornell University Press, 1982.

8 These connections are explored in greater detail in Csikszentmihalyi, Mihaly, and Rick Emery Robinson. *The Art of Seeing: An Interpretation of the Aesthetic Encounter*. Malibu, Calif. : Los Angeles, Calif: J.P. Getty Museum ; Getty Center for Education in the Arts, 1990.

9 Jensen, Michael C., and William H. Meckling. "Theory of the Firm: Managerial Behavior, Agency Costs and Ownership Structure." *Journal of Financial Economics* 3, no. 4 (October 1976): 305–60.

10 Galtung, Johan. "Anomie/Atomie: On the Impact of Secularization/Modernization on Moral Cohesion and Social Tissue." *International Journal of Sociology and Social Policy* 15, no. 8/9/10 (August 1, 1995): 121–47.

11 Dunbar, R. I. M. *How Many Friends Does One Person Need? Dunbar's Number and Other Evolutionary Quirks.* Cambridge, Mass: Harvard University Press, 2010.

12 As an example, CauseIQ states that 85.1% of all nonprofits have no employees at all, but only volunteers: Cause IQ. "2019 Nonprofit Employment Statistics." Accessed April 9, 2021. https://www.causeiq.com/insights/nonprofit-employment-stats-2019/.

13 In one study, Woong Jo Chang found that almost 84 percent of arts organizations in the Columbus, Ohio, metropolitan area had five or fewer employees: Chang, Woong Jo. "How 'Small' Are Small Arts Organizations?" *Journal of Arts Management, Law, and Society* 40 (2010): 217–34.

14 Dworkin, Aaron P. "Closing Keynote Address." Presented at the Emerging Arts Leaders Symposium (EALS), American University, Washington, DC, April 7, 2013.

15 "Poet Laureate: Billy Collins." PBS NewsHour, December 10, 2001. https://www.pbs.org/newshour/show/poet-laureate-billy-collins.

16 Plimpton, George. "Billy Collins, The Art of Poetry No. 83." *The Paris Review,* 2001. https://www.theparisreview.org/interviews/482/the-art-of-poetry-no-83-billy-collins.

17 Rose, Daniel Asa. "Billy Collins Gleefully Needles Opaque Poets." *Observer.* October 4, 2016. https://observer.com/2016/10/billy-collins-gleefully-needles-opaque-poets/.

18 Adizes, Ichak. *Leading the Leaders: How to Enrich Your Style of Management and Handle People Whose Style Is Different from Yours.* The Adizes Institute Publishing, 2004.

19 Scharmer, C. Otto. *Theory U: Leading from the Future as It Emerges.* Second Edition. Oakland, CA: Berrett-Koehler, 2016.

20 Argyris, Chris. *Overcoming Organizational Defenses: Facilitating Organizational Learning.* Boston: Allyn and Bacon, 1990.

21 Becker, Howard S. *Art Worlds*. 25th anniversary edition. Berkeley: University of California Press, 2008.

22 Eagleton, Terry. *The Ideology of the Aesthetic*. Cambridge, MA, USA: Basil Blackwell, 1990.

23 Dobson, John. "Aesthetics as a Foundation for Business Activity." *Journal of Business Ethics* 72, no. 1 (April 1, 2007): 41–46.

24 Janson, H. W. *History of Art : A Survey of the Major Visual Arts from the Dawn of History to the Present Day*. Revised and Enlarged Edition 1969 / 15th Printing Oct 1970. Englewood Cliffs, NJ: Prentice Hall, Inc., 1963.

25 Polanyi, Michael, and Harry Prosch. *Meaning*. Chicago: University of Chicago Press, 1975.

26 Forster, E. M. "Art for Art's Sake." *Harper's Magazine*, August 1, 1949.

27 Klinkenborg, Verlyn. *Several Short Sentences about Writing*. New York: Vintage Books, 2012.

28 Dickson, Paul. *New Dickson Baseball Dictionary.* Harcourt Brace & Company, 1999.

29 King, Alexandra. "The Aesthetic Attitude." *The Internet Encyclopedia of Philosophy*, ISSN 2161-0002, https://iep.utm.edu/aesth-at/.

30 Bullough, Edward. "Psychical Distance as a Factor in Art and an Aesthetic Principle." *British Journal of Psychology*; London, Etc. 5, no. 2 (June 1, 1912): 87–118.

31 McCauley, Cynthia D., Wilfred H. Drath, Charles J. Palus, Patricia M. G. O'Connor, and Becca A. Baker. "The Use of Constructive-Developmental Theory to Advance the Understanding of Leadership." *The Leadership Quarterly*, 17, no. 6 (December 1, 2006): 634–53.

32 These four categories were stolen, brazenly, from Adrian Ellis and his briefing paper for the June 2003 conference on "Valuing Culture" hosted by Demos. PDF of Adrian's article available at: http://www.demos.co.uk/files/File/VACUAEllis.pdf

33 McCarthy, Kevin F., Elizabeth H. Ondaatje, Laura Zakaras, and Arthur Brooks. *Gifts of the Muse: Reframing the Debate About the Benefits of the Arts*. RAND Corporation, 2004. http://www.rand.org/pubs/monographs/MG218.html.

34 Mintzberg, Henry. *Rebalancing Society: Radical Renewal Beyond Left, Right, and Center*. 1st edition. Berrett-Koehler Publishers, 2015.

35 This quote is often attributed to Albert Einstein, but is actually a restatement of Einstein's ideas by composer George Sessions. The best evidence of the original quote is in Einstein, Albert. 1934. "On the Method of Theoretical Physics." *Philosophy of Science* 1 (2): 165. Session's reimagining of the idea is in Sessions, Roger. 1950. "How a 'Difficult' Composer Gets That Way." *The New York Times*, January 8, 1950: 89.

36 Walker, Alissa. "Interview with Bill McDonough." Dwell. Accessed March 19, 2021. https://www.dwell.com/article/interview-with-bill-mcdonough-e1d42751.

37 Hansmann, Henry. *The Ownership of Enterprise*. Cambridge, Mass: The Belknap Press of Harvard University Press, 1996.

38 Jensen, Michael C., and William H. Meckling. "Theory of the Firm: Managerial Behavior, Agency Costs and Ownership Structure." *Journal of Financial Economics* 3, no. 4 (October 1976): 305–60.

39 Cyert, Richard Michael, and James G. March. *A Behavioral Theory of the Firm*. 2nd ed. Cambridge, Mass., USA: Blackwell Business, 1992.

40 Tippett, Krista. "Pádraig Ó Tuama – Belonging Creates and Undoes Us." On Being. March 2, 2017. https://onbeing.org/programs/padraig-o-tuama-belonging-creates-and-undoes-us/.

41 Liechty, Joseph, and Cecelia Clegg. *Moving Beyond Sectarianism: Religion, Conflict, and Reconciliation in Northern Ireland*. Dublin, Ireland: Columba Press, 2001.

42 Leopold, Aldo. *A Sand County Almanac*. 7th printing edition. New York: Ballantine Books, 1986.

43 Penny, Laura. *Your Call Is Important to Us: The Truth About Bullshit.* New York: Crown, 2005.

44 The quote is attributed to many different individuals, from Steve Martin to Frank Zappa to Laurie Anderson. Quote Investigator determined that the first published version is attributed to actor/comedian Martin Mull: https://quoteinvestigator.com/2010/11/08/writing-about-music/.

45 Granma International, English Edition, October 29, 2005.

46 Meadows, Donella. "Indicators and Information Systems for Sustainable Development." The Sustainability Institute, 1998.

47 Dewey, John. *Art as Experience.* New York: Minton, Balch & Company, 1934.

48 Heisenberg, Werner. *Physics and Philosophy: The Revolution in Modern Science.* 1st ed. World Perspectives, v. 19. New York: Harper, 1958.

49 Simon, Herbert A. "Rational Decision Making in Business Organizations." *The American Economic Review* 69, no. 4 (September 1, 1979): 493–513.

50 Mintzberg, Henry, Duru Raisinghani, and André Théorêt. "The Structure of 'Unstructured' Decision Processes." *Administrative Science Quarterly* 21, no. 2 (June 1, 1976): 246–75.

51 Robinson, Ken. "Do Schools Kill Creativity?" TED, 2006. https://tinyurl.com/sirkenonschools.

52 Strati, Antonio. *Organization and Aesthetics.* London ; Thousand Oaks, Calif: SAGE, 1999.

53 Government of Ireland. Taxes Consolidation Act, 1997, 39 § 195 (1997). http://www.irishstatutebook.ie/eli/1997/act/39/section/195/enacted/en/html#zza39y1997s195.

54 ArtSpace website: https://www.artspace.org/.

55 Brockman, John. "The Adjacent Possible: A Talk with Stuart A. Kauffman." Edge, November 9, 2003. https://www.edge.org/conversation/stuart_a_kauffman-the-adjacent-possible.

56 Johnson, Steven. *Where Good Ideas Come From: The Natural History of Innovation*. 1st edition. New York: Riverhead Books, 2010.

57 Snowden, David. "Complexity, Citizen Engagement in a Post-Social Media Time." TEDx Talks, 2018. https://www.youtube.com/watch?v=JkJDyPh9phc.

58 Loewenstein, George. "The Psychology of Curiosity: A Review and Reinterpretation." *Psychological Bulletin* July 1994 116, no. 1 (1994): 75–98.

59 See, for example, seven psychological functions of art suggested in Botton, Alain de, and John Armstrong. *Art as Therapy*. Illustrated edition. London: Phaidon Press, 2013.

60 For more on Pacioli and his relationship with da Vinci, see Gleeson-White, Jane. *Double Entry: How the Merchants of Venice Created Modern Finance*. 1 edition. New York: W. W. Norton & Company, 2012.

61 DeVereaux, Constance, and Pekka Vartiainen, eds. *The Science and Art of Cultural Management. Cultural Management and the State of the Field*. Helsinki, Finland: HUMAK, 2009. For more on arts management as a "borrower's field," see Brindle, Meg, and Constance DeVereaux. *The Arts Management Handbook: New Directions for Students and Practitioners*. M.E. Sharpe, 2011.

62 Gartner, W.B. (1990). "What are we talking about when we talk about entrepreneurship?" *Journal of Business Venturing* 5(1): 15–28.

63 The remaining theme in Gartner's list, Profit or Nonprofit, captured the continuing discussion of whether entrepreneurship was purely profit-focused, or could have other goals as well...suggesting a theme that is about person, process, and outcome all at once.

64 Ackoff, R.L. (1973). "Science in the systems age: Beyond IE, OR, and MS." *Operations Research* 21(3): 661–71.

65 Bruyat, C., & Julien, P-A. (2001). "Defining the field of research in entrepreneurship." *Journal of Business Venturing* 16(2): 165–80.

66 Shirky, Clay. "Institutions vs. Collaboration." TEDGlobal, 2005. https://www.ted.com/talks/clay_shirky_institutions_vs_collaboration .

67 See, for example, Overholser, George M. "Nonprofit Growth Capital: Defining, Measuring and Managing Growth Capital in Nonprofit Enterprises." Nonprofit Finance Fund, 2010. http://nonprofitfinancefund.org/capital-services/builders-vs-buyers.

68 Curtis, Elizabeth Cabral. "National Capitalization Project 2010 Summary." Grantmakers in the Arts, September 2010.

ABOUT THE AUTHOR

E. Andrew Taylor thinks (a bit too much) about organizational structure, strategy, and management practice in the nonprofit arts. An Associate Professor of Arts Management at American University in Washington, DC, he also consults for cultural, educational, and support organizations.

Since July 2003, he has shared what he learns at "The Artful Manager" (www.artfulmanager.com), where the original drafts of this book's 50 chapters first appeared.

Andrew lives in Maryland with his brilliant wife, Ximena, and two glorious step-children, Sol and Joaquin. His two grown-up children, Abby and Sam, are out in the world making it significantly more beautiful and more kind.

Photo by Ximena Varela

Made in United States
North Haven, CT
27 September 2022

24624898R00117